My Country 'tis of Thee
A Picture Book of America

Series I, Volume 1
Solano County California
by Sharon Chestang-Robinson

Sharing pictures of our U.S. of A. Unspoiled Sonoma County, California. A series of nostalgic pictures of Vallejo, American Canyon, Birds Landing, Pantano, Suisun City, Fairfield, and Vacaville. Nestled in the heart of Northern California offering great wine, vineyards, country homes and yards, unique wildlife, arts and crafts, weather, rolling hills and grasslands, community, sunsets, and an uncongested lifestyle of relaxation.

This book belongs to:

_____

If found, please return to:

_____

Dedicated to our North American land, and to those
who want to see and enjoy more of it. Thank you.

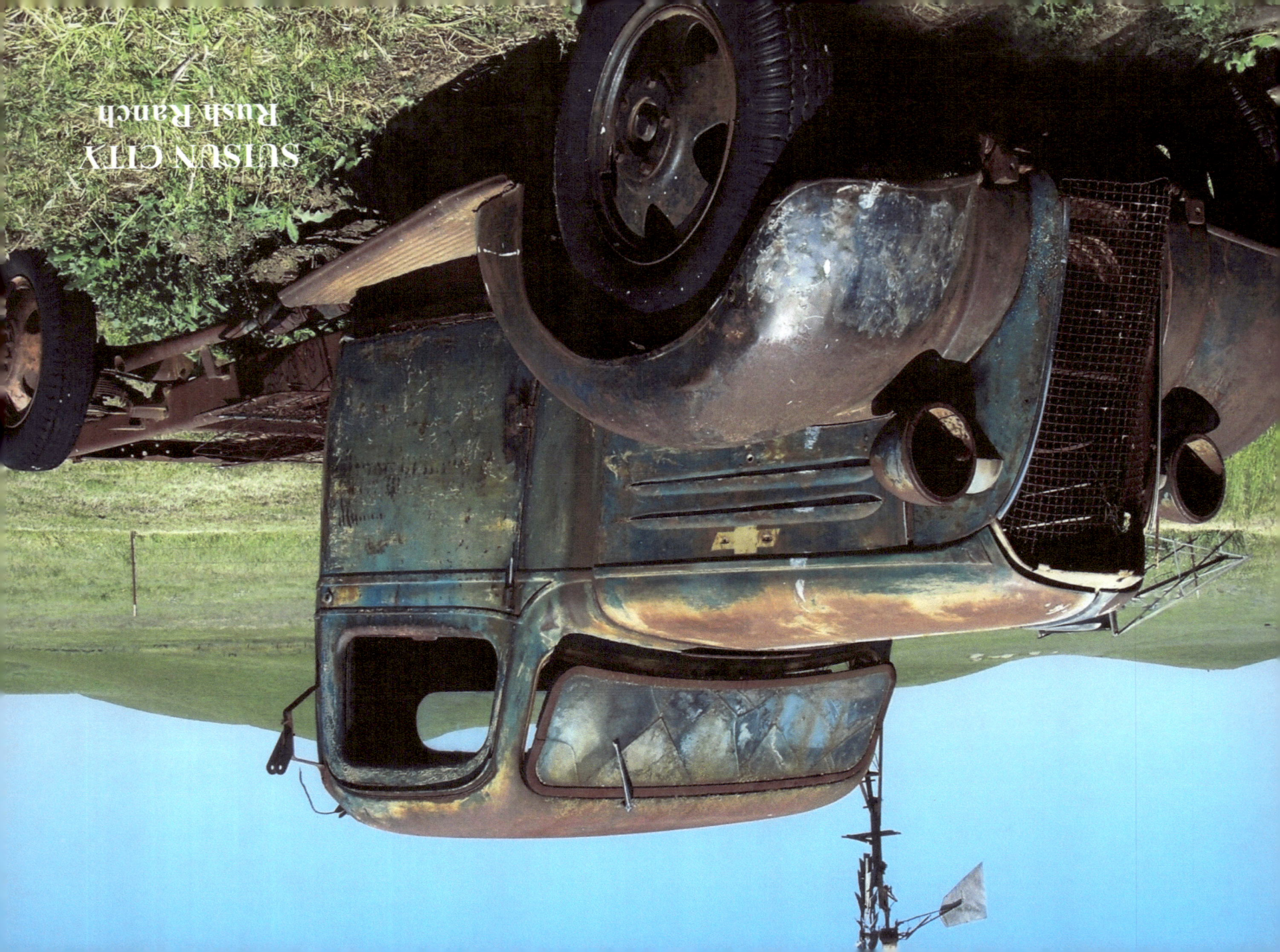

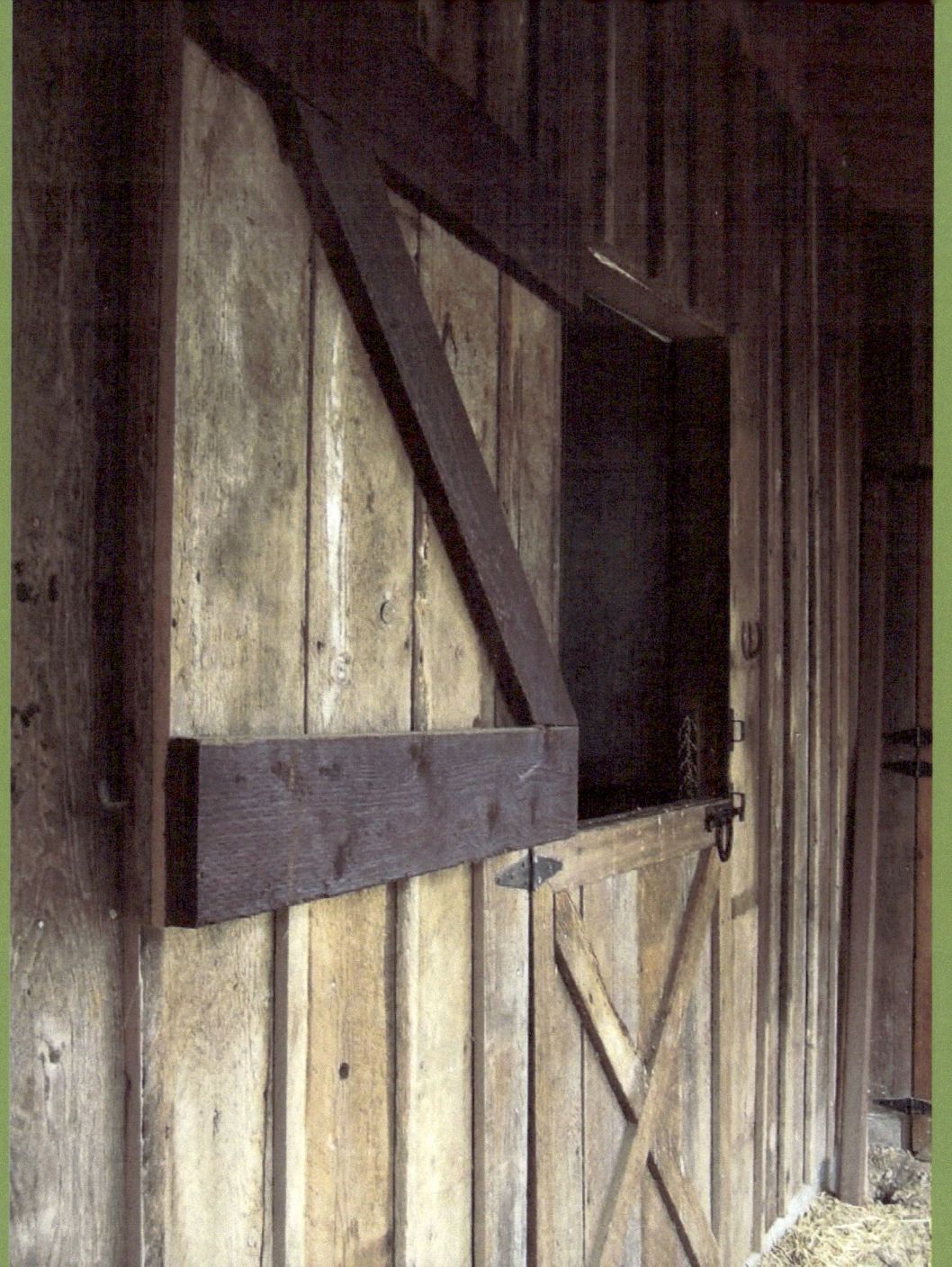

SUISUN CITY
Rush Ranch

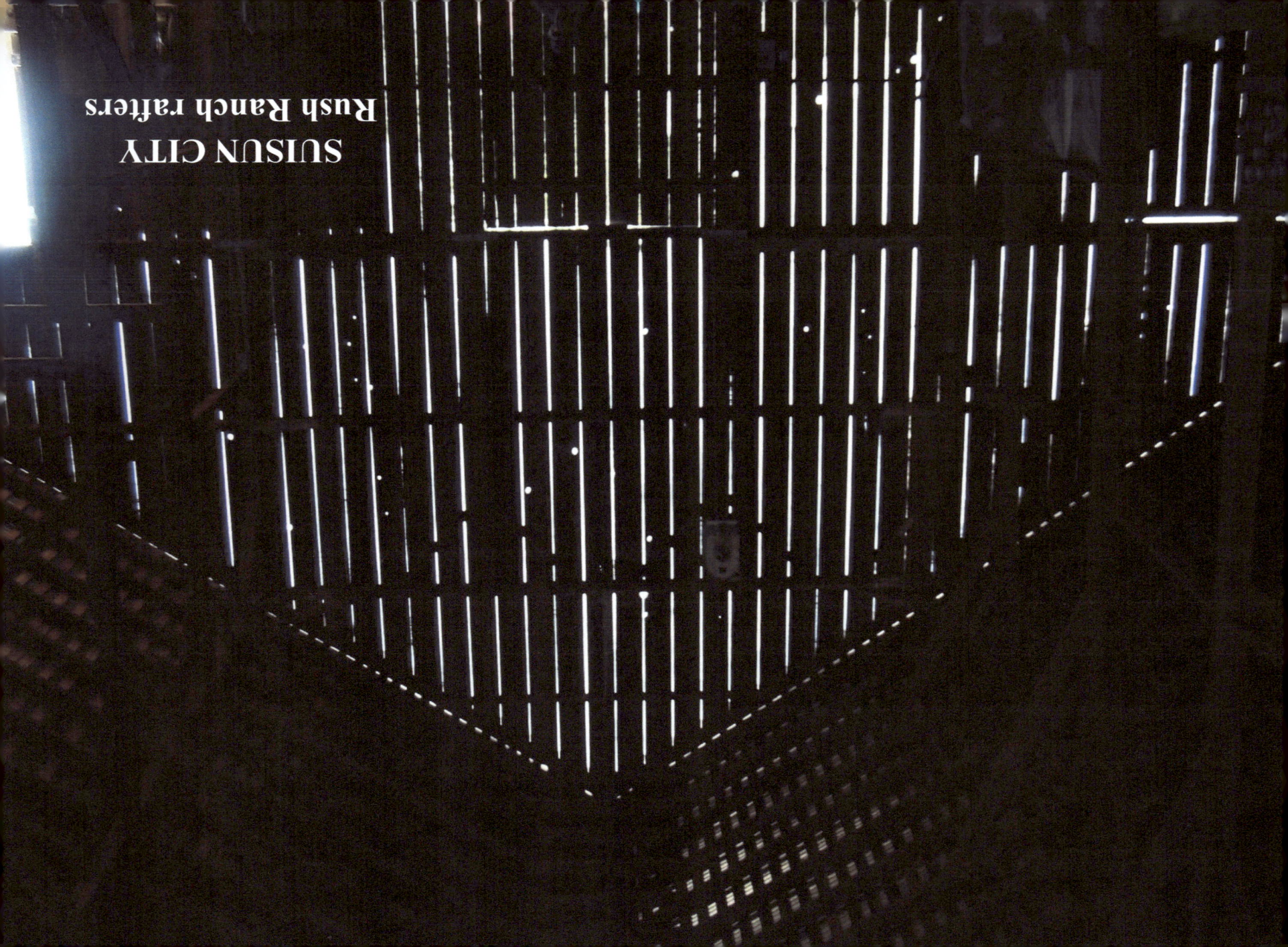

SUISUN CITY
Rush Ranch rafters

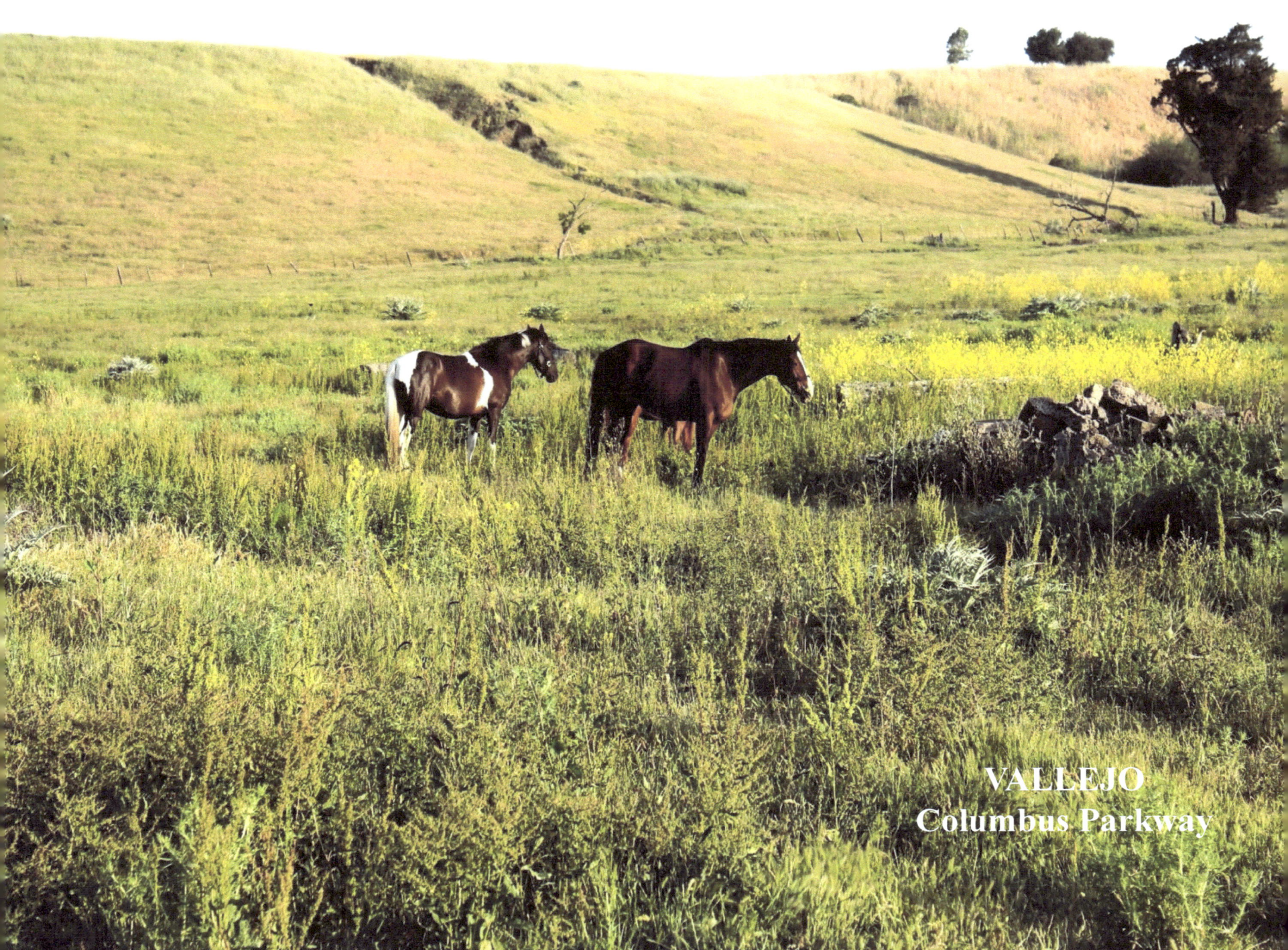

VALLEJO
Columbus Parkway

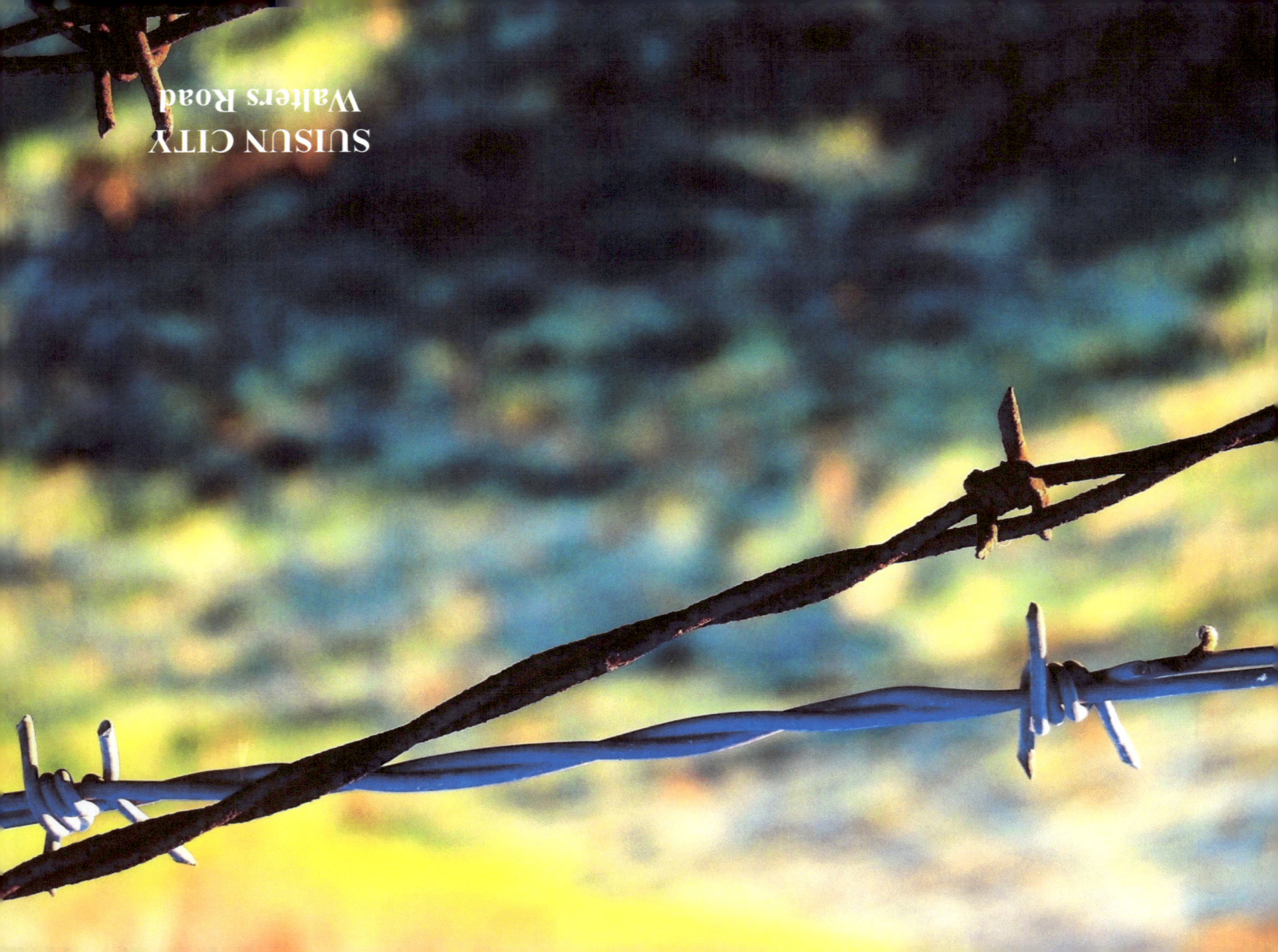

SUISUN CITY
Walters Road

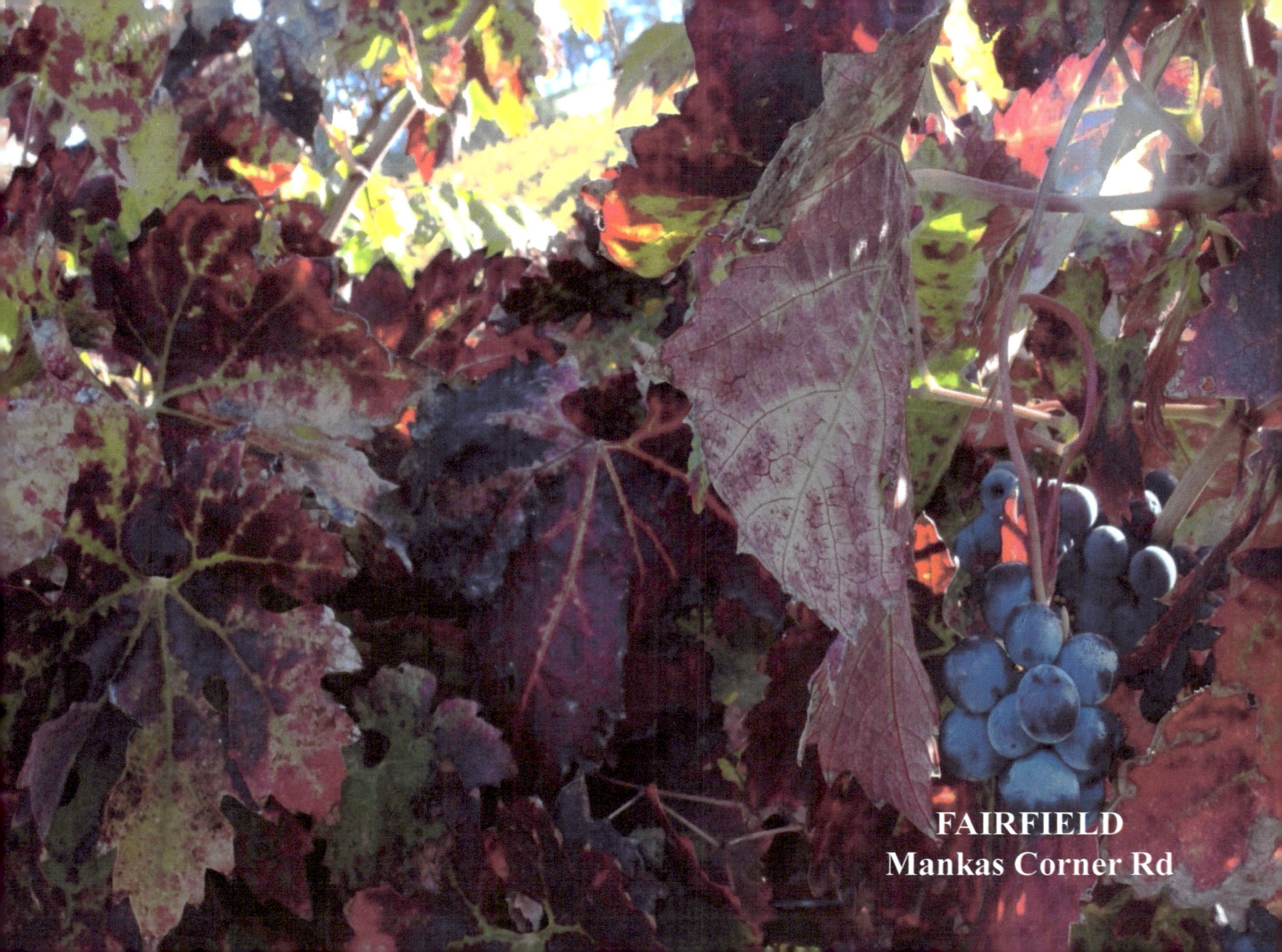

FAIRFIELD
Mankas Corner Rd

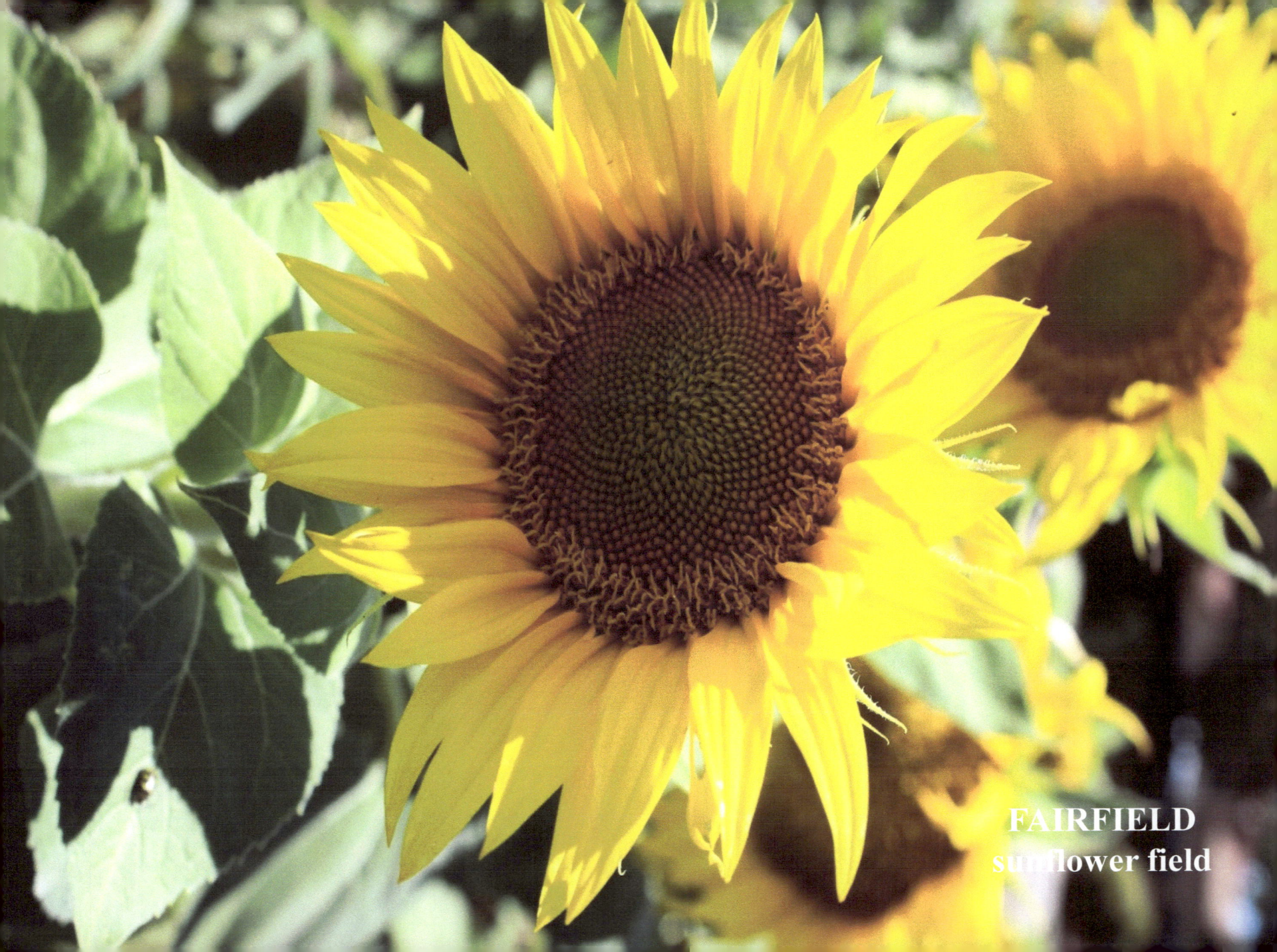

FAIRFIELD
sunflower field

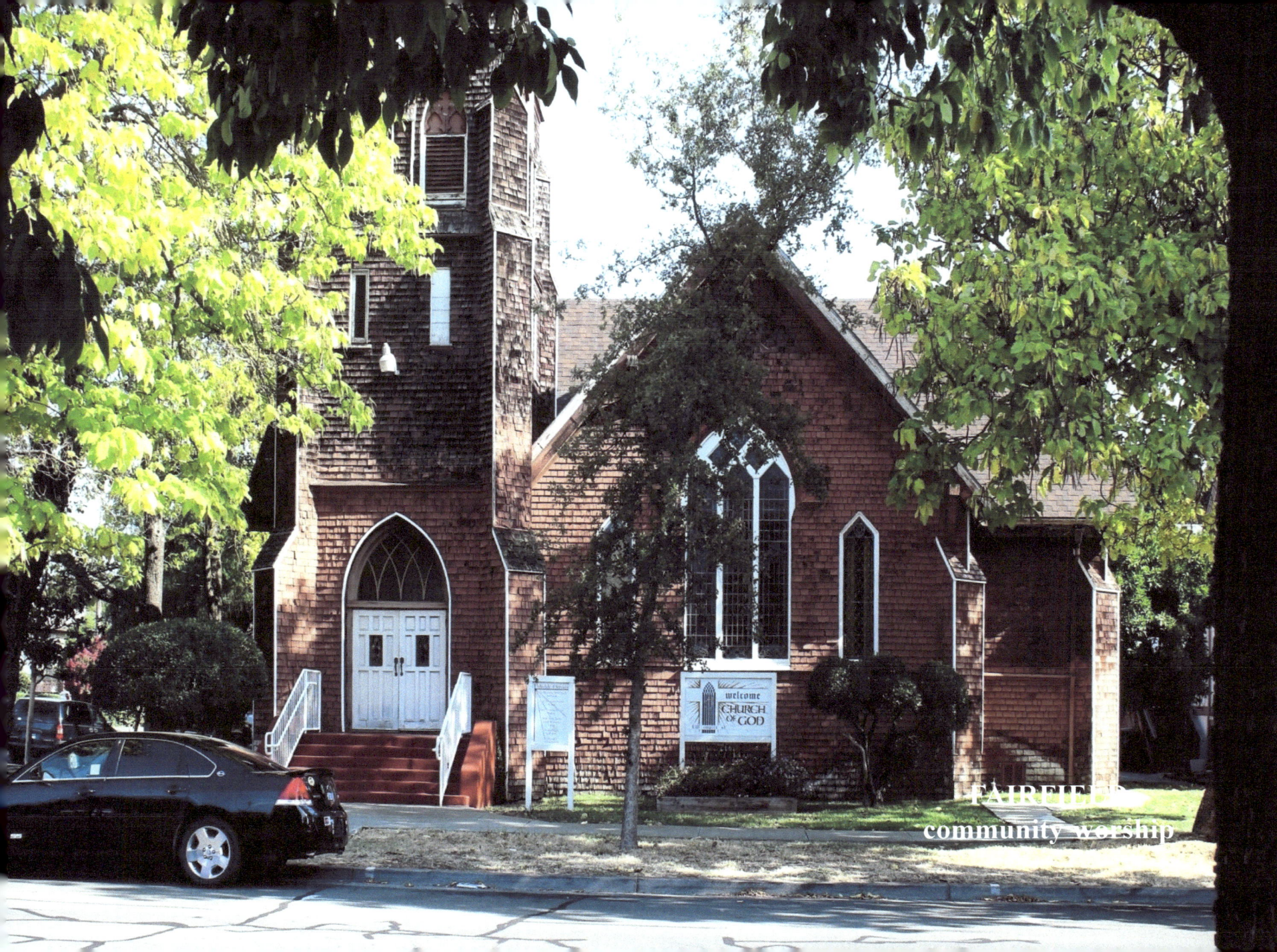

FAIRFIELD
community worship

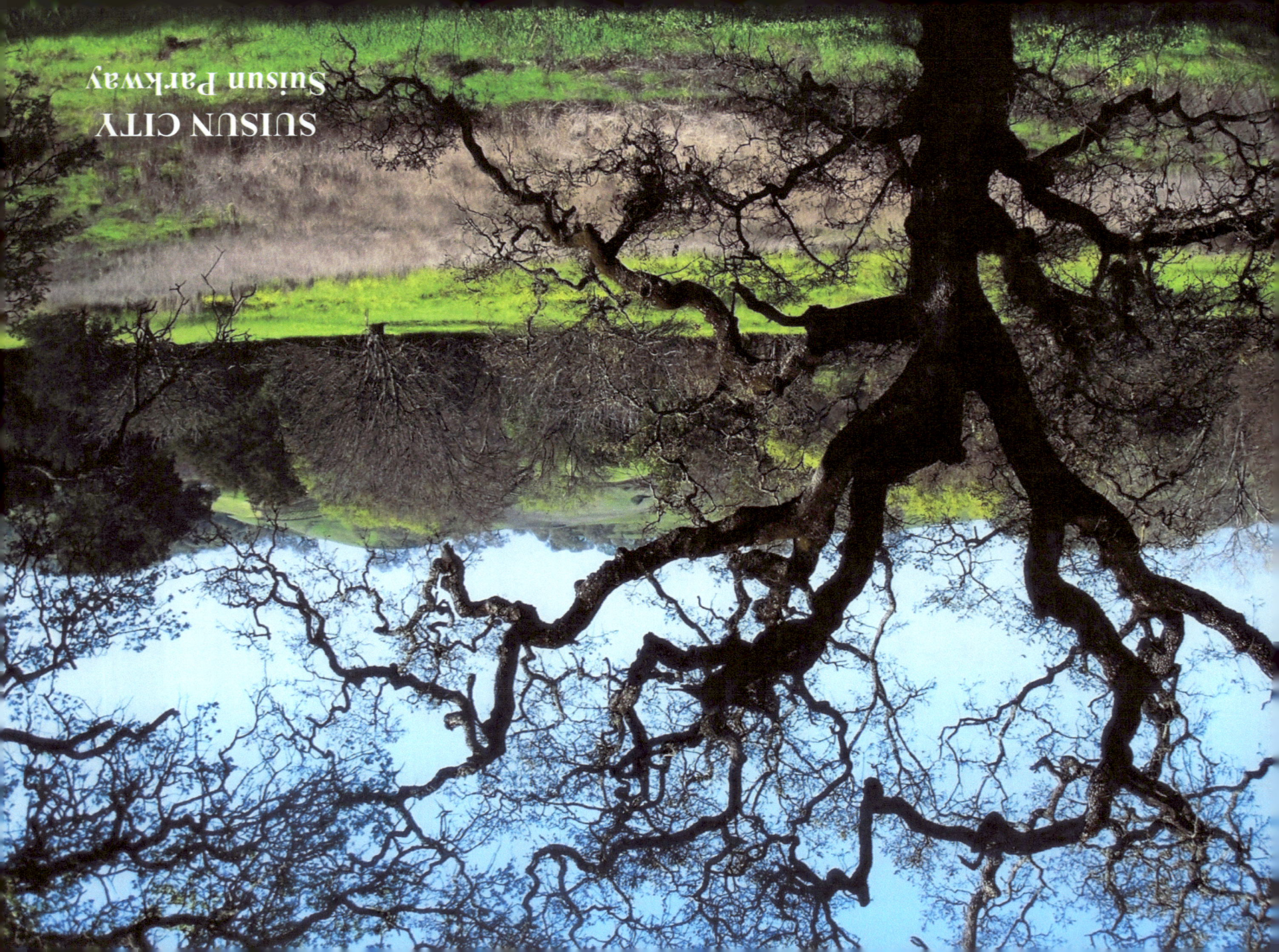

SUISUN CITY
Suisun Parkway

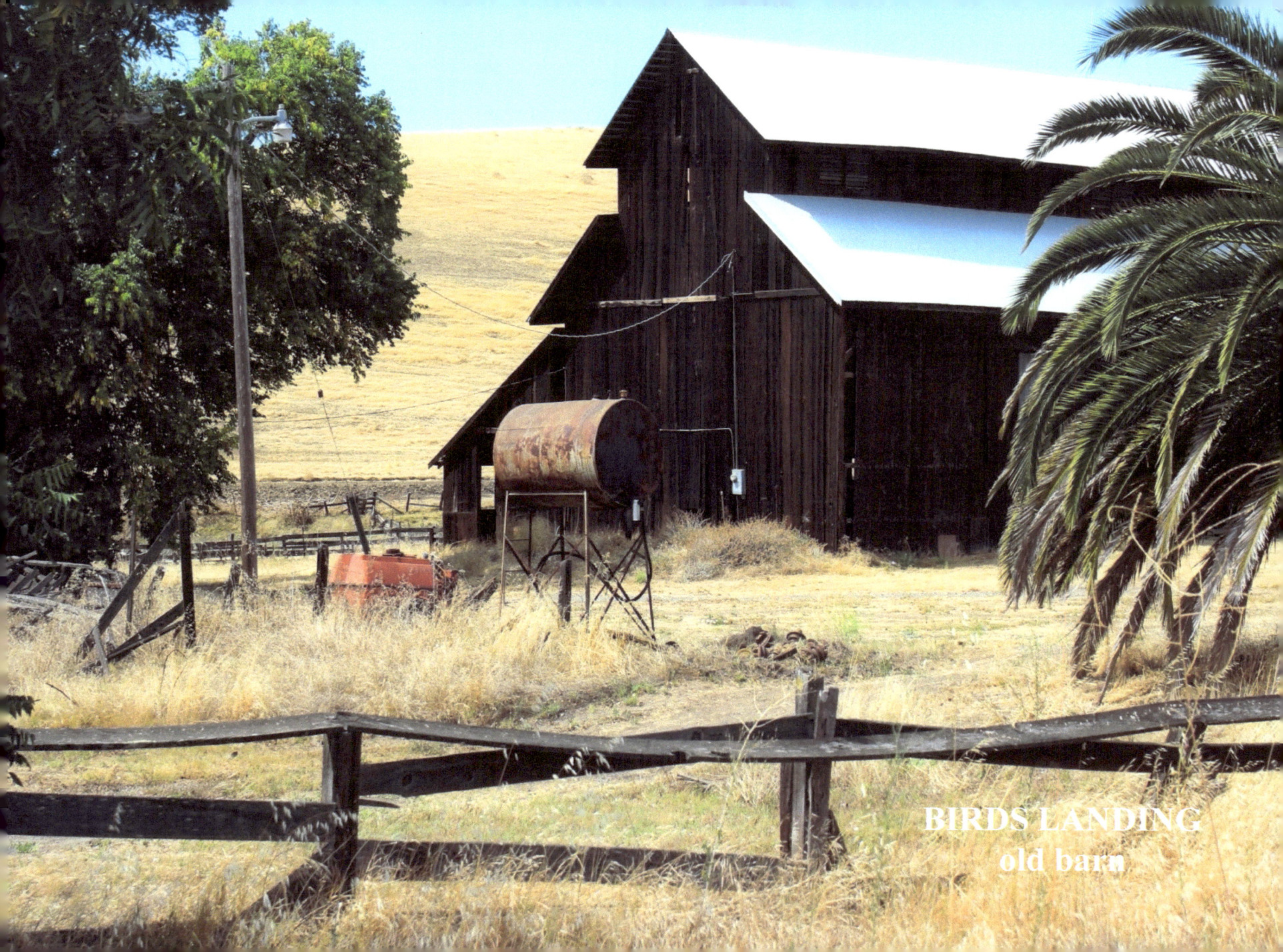

BIRDS LANDING
old barn

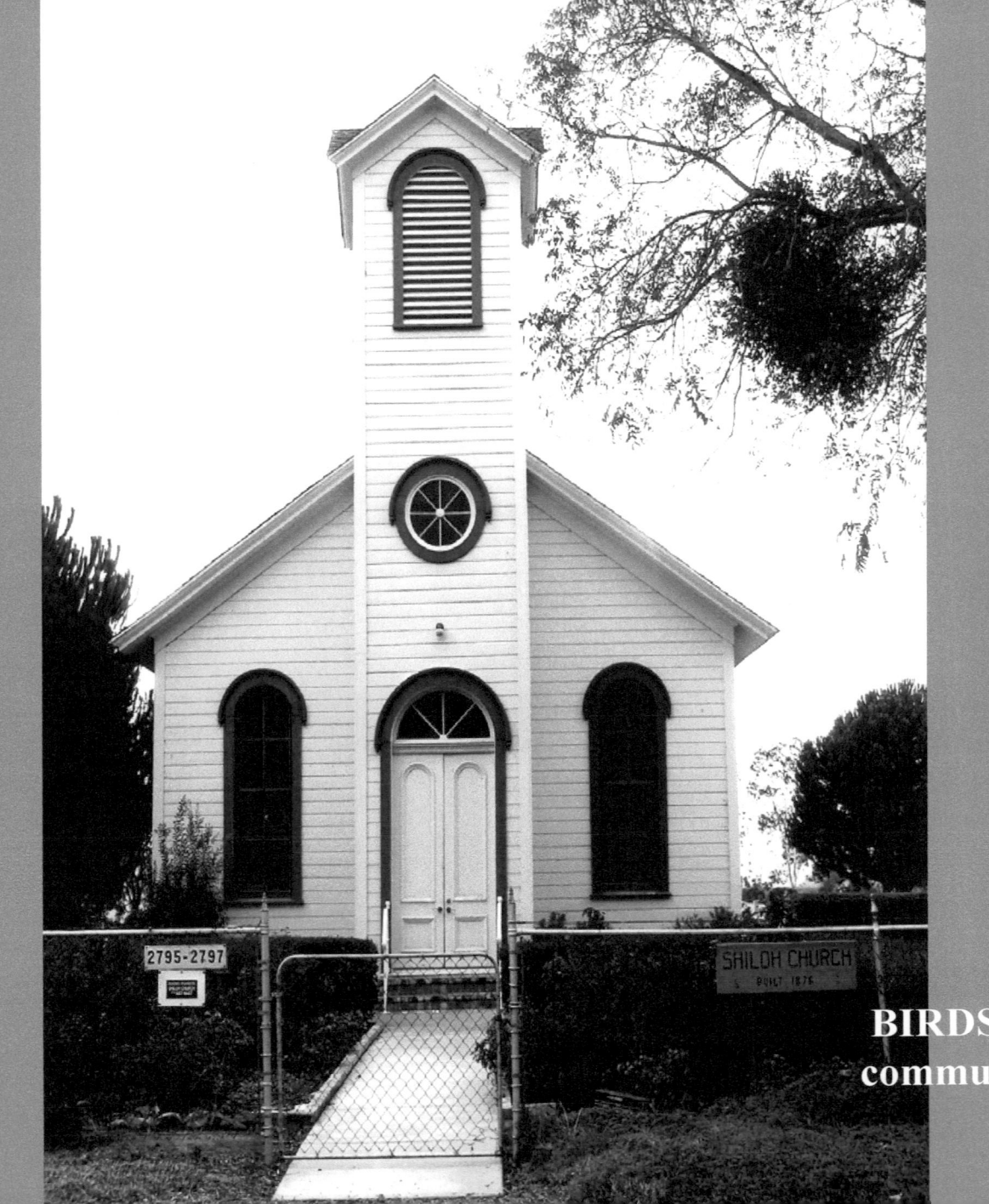

BIRDS LANDING
community worship

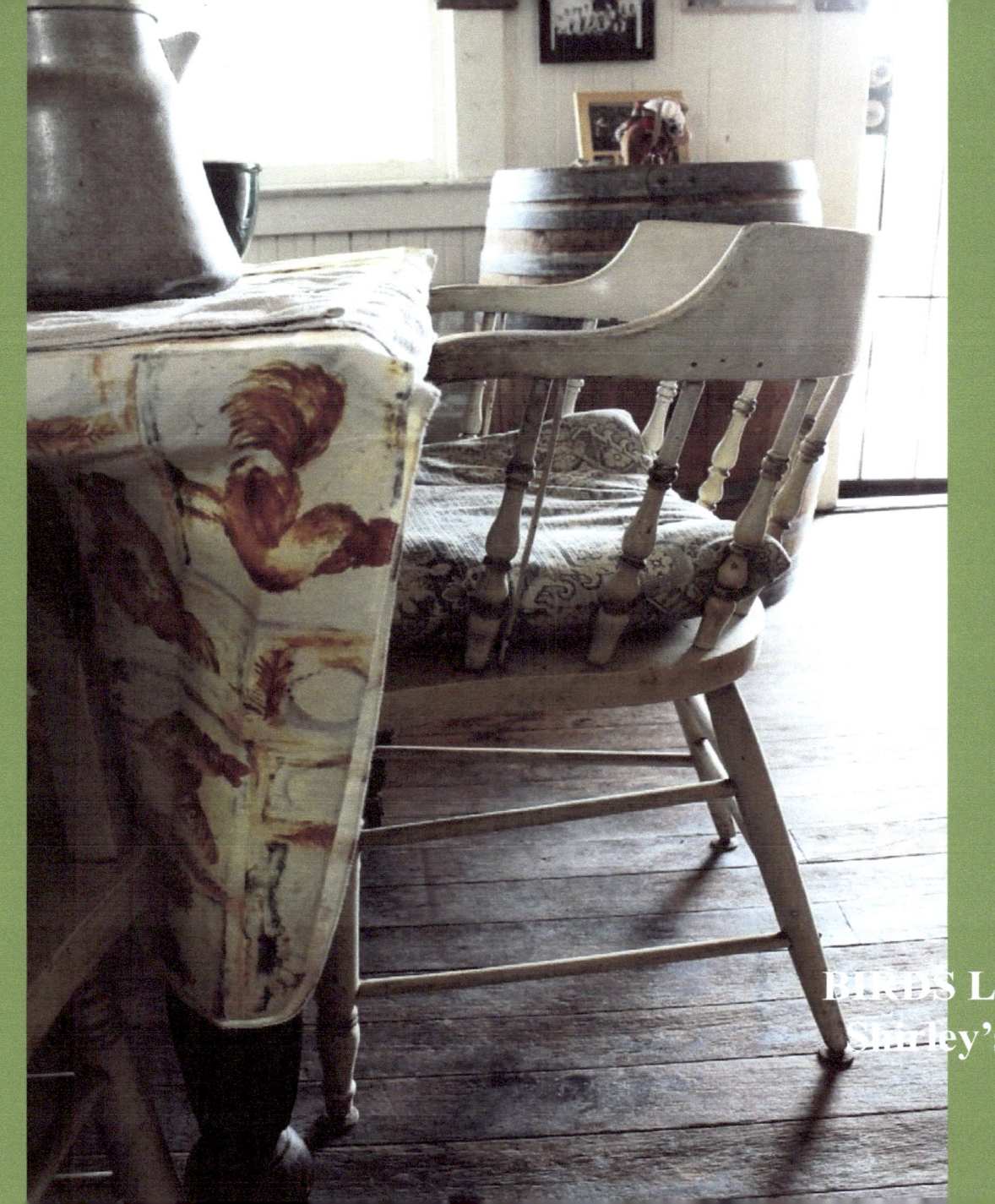

BIRDS LANDING
Shirley's Tavern

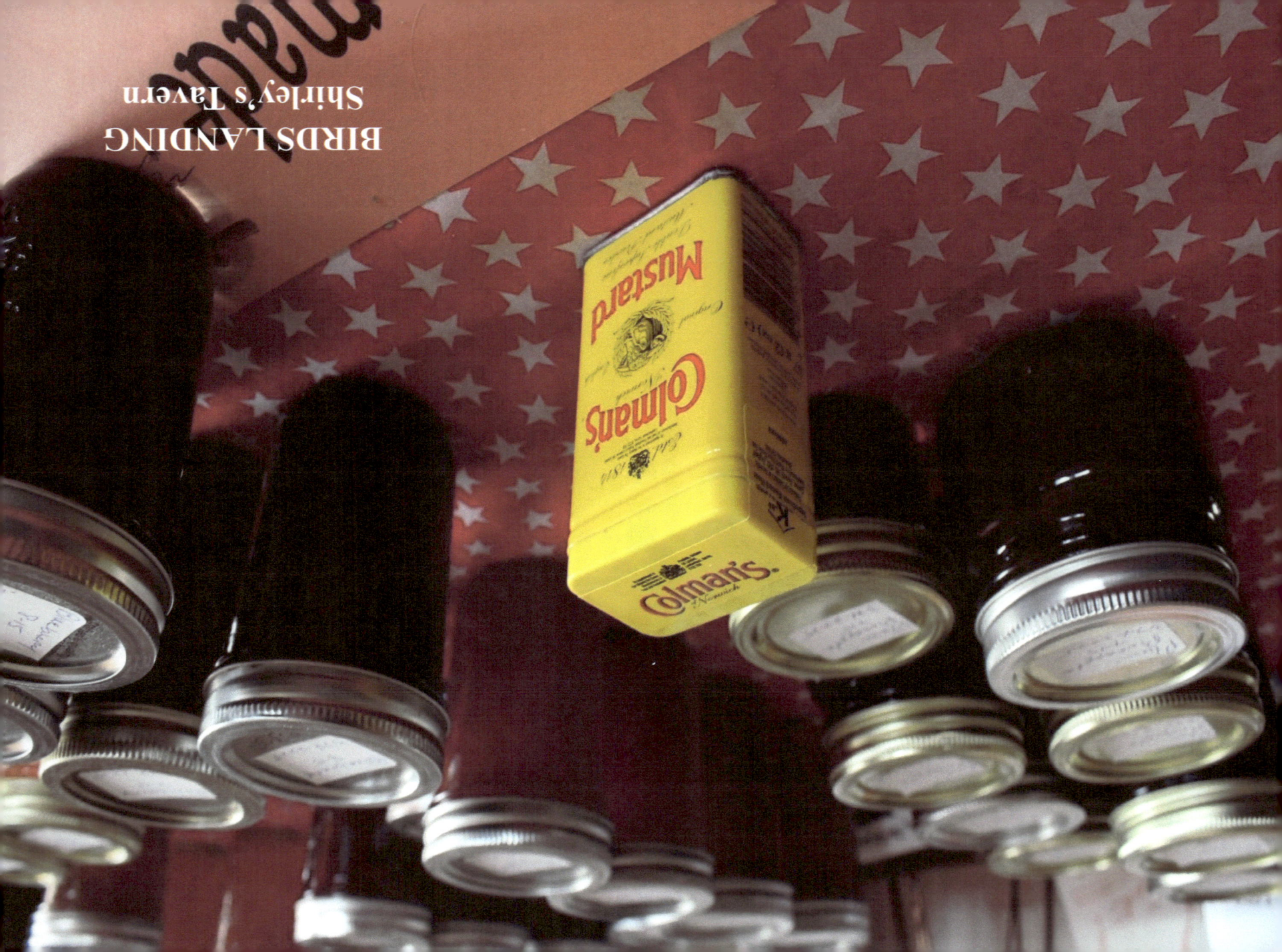

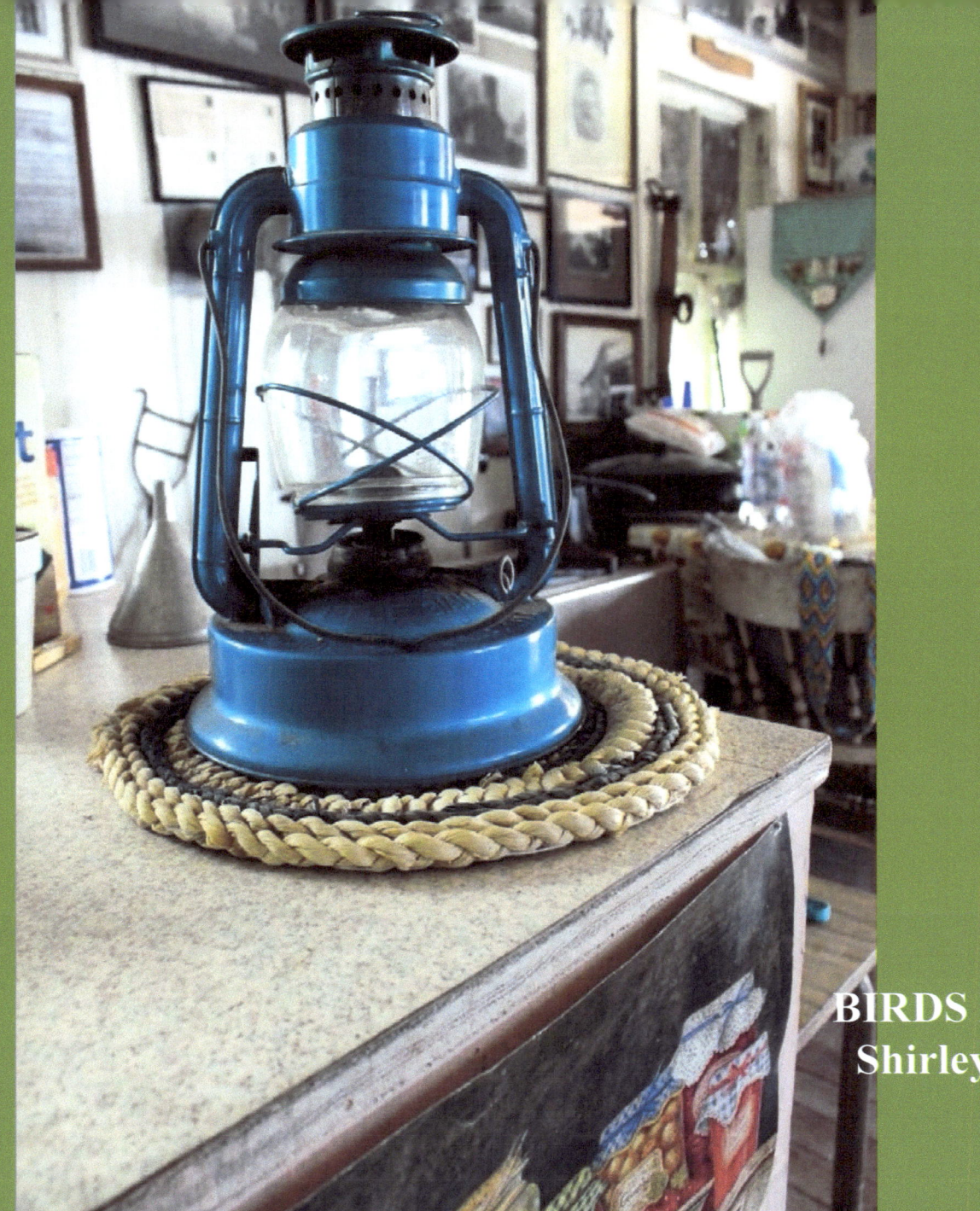

BIRDS LANDING
Shirley's Tavern

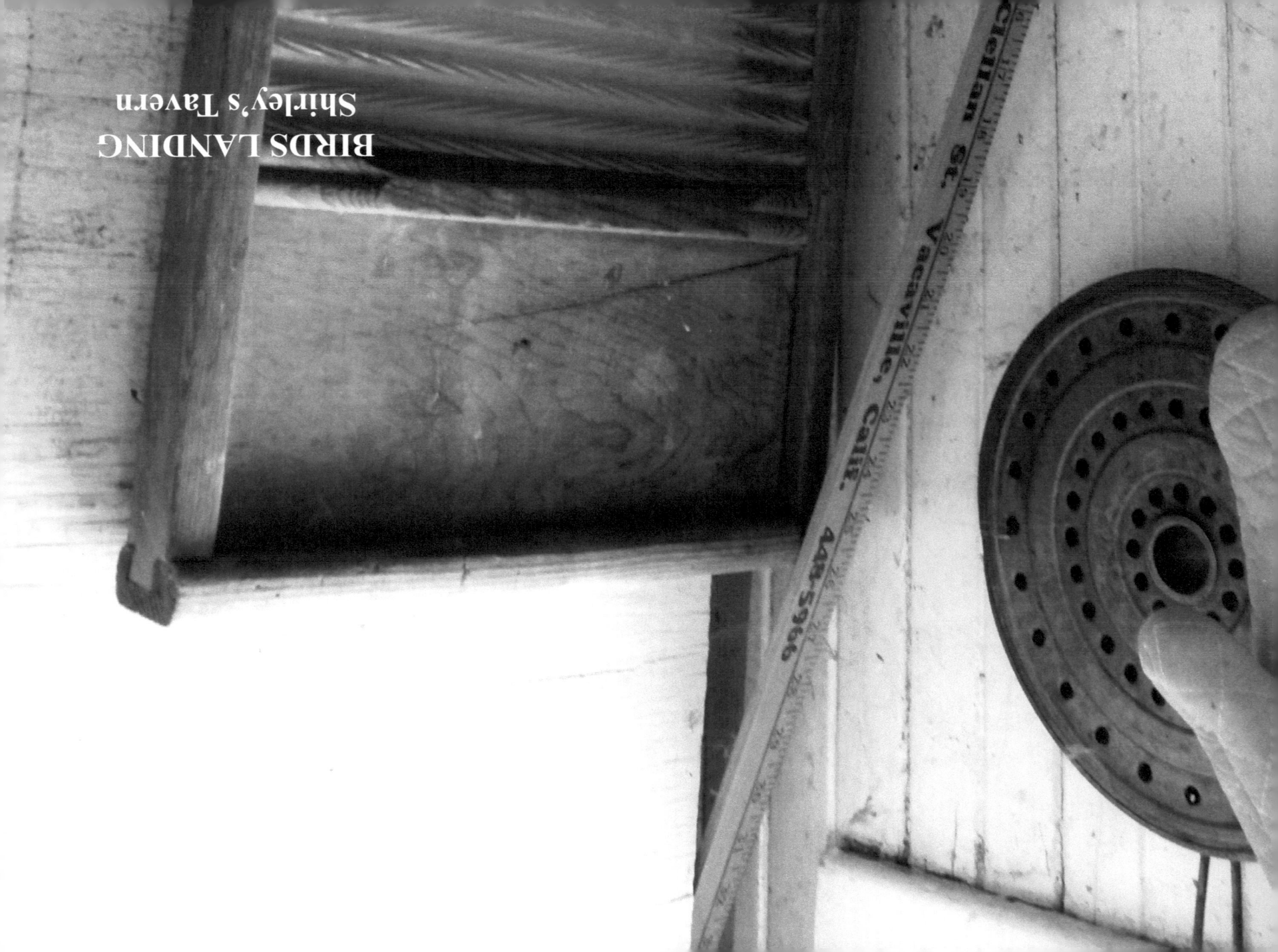

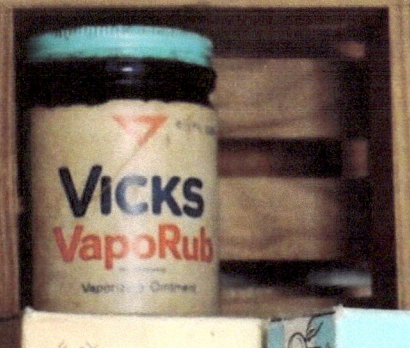

VICKS VapoRub

THE ORIGINAL Faultles STARCH

SINCE 1887

Easiest Starch to Iron the Way You Want to Look

NET WT 12 OZ (340 GRAMS)

Faultless

BLUED & PERFUMED starch

Good Housekeeping

NET WT 12 OZ (340 GRAMS)

designed for today's fabrics and fashions

LUX SOAP FLAKES

Easy care for Wash'n Wear and all fine fabrics

BOI AXO Powdered Hand Soap

CLEANS dirty HANDS

BIRDS LANDING
Shirley's Tavern

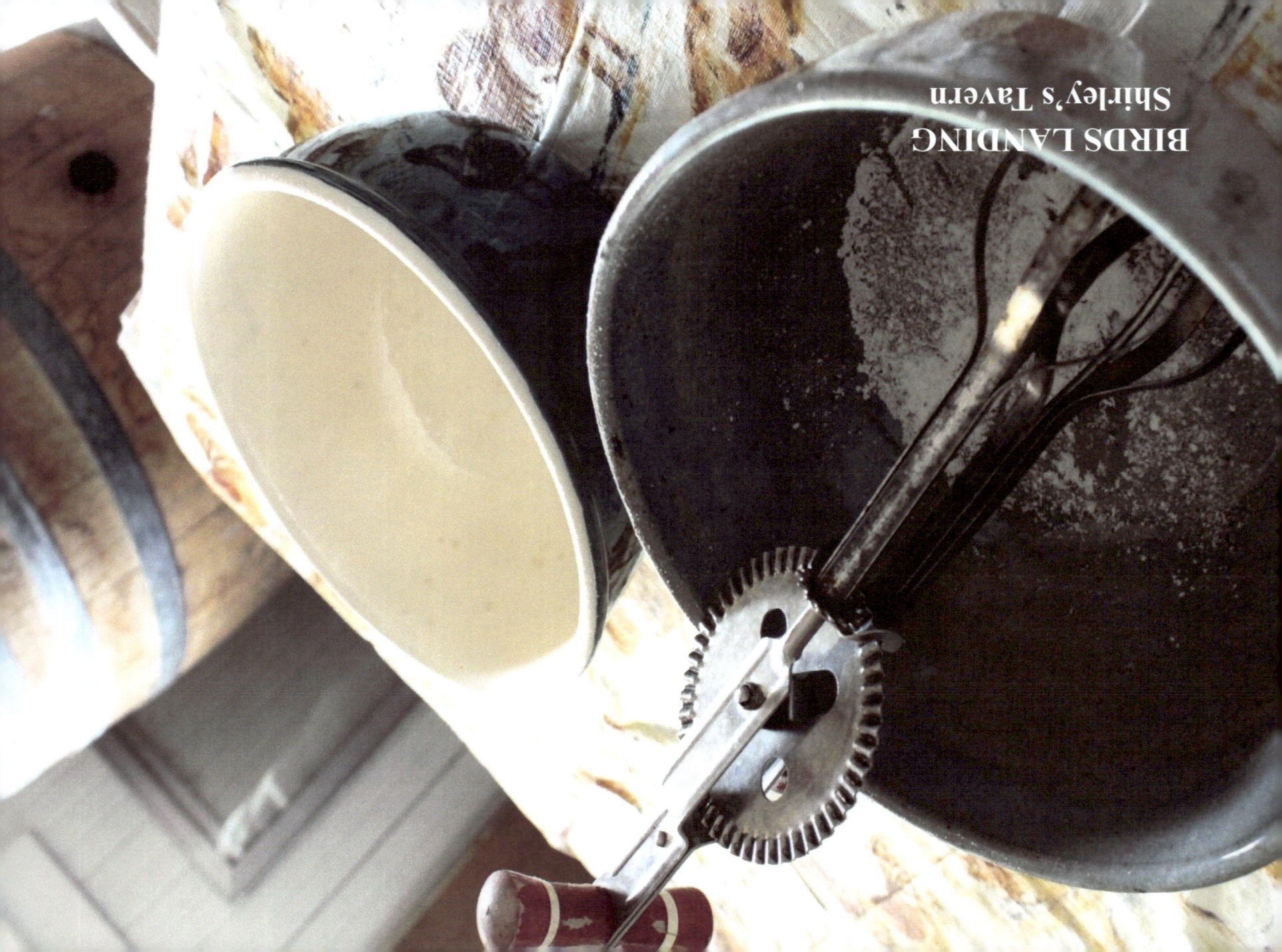

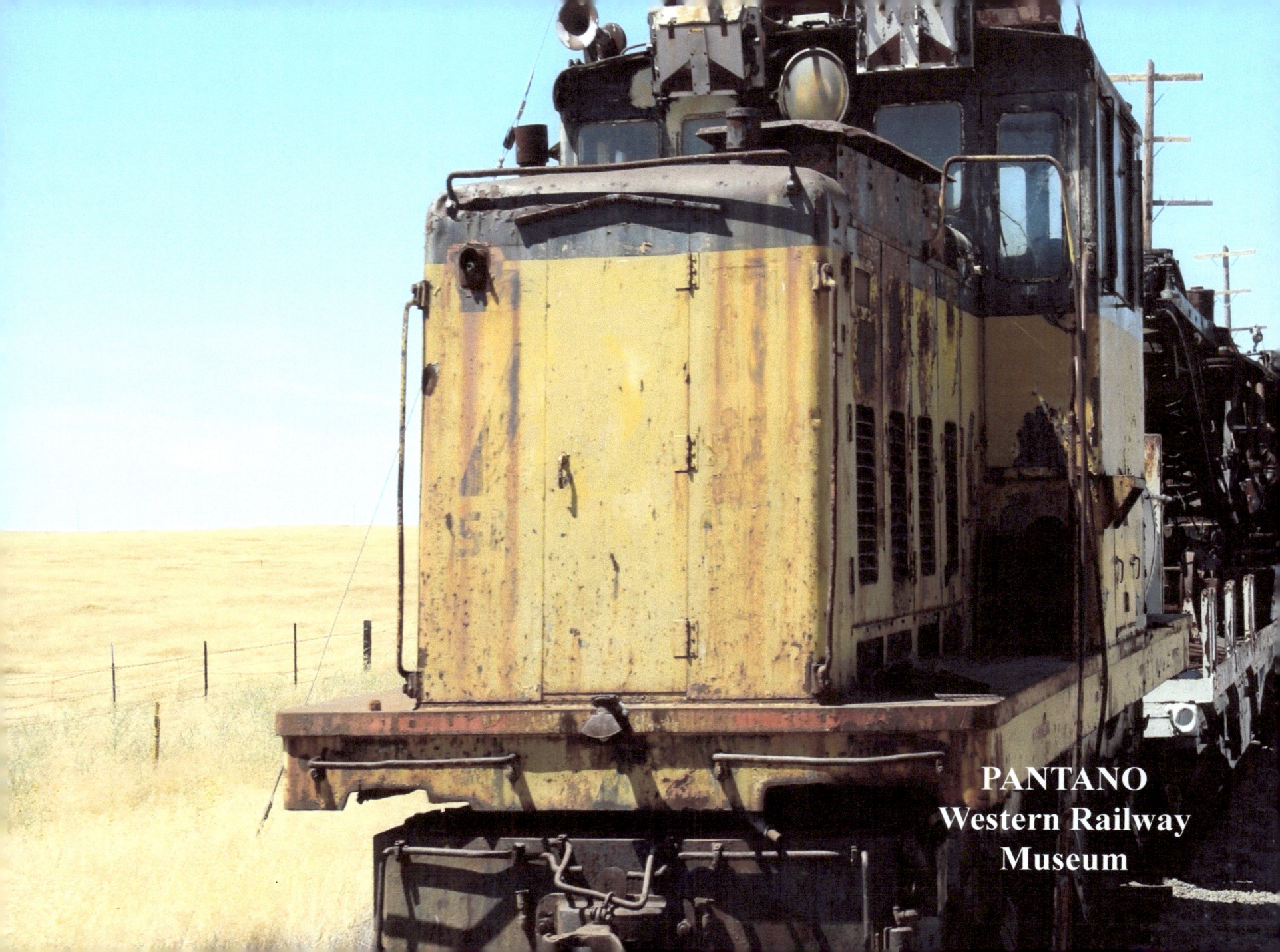

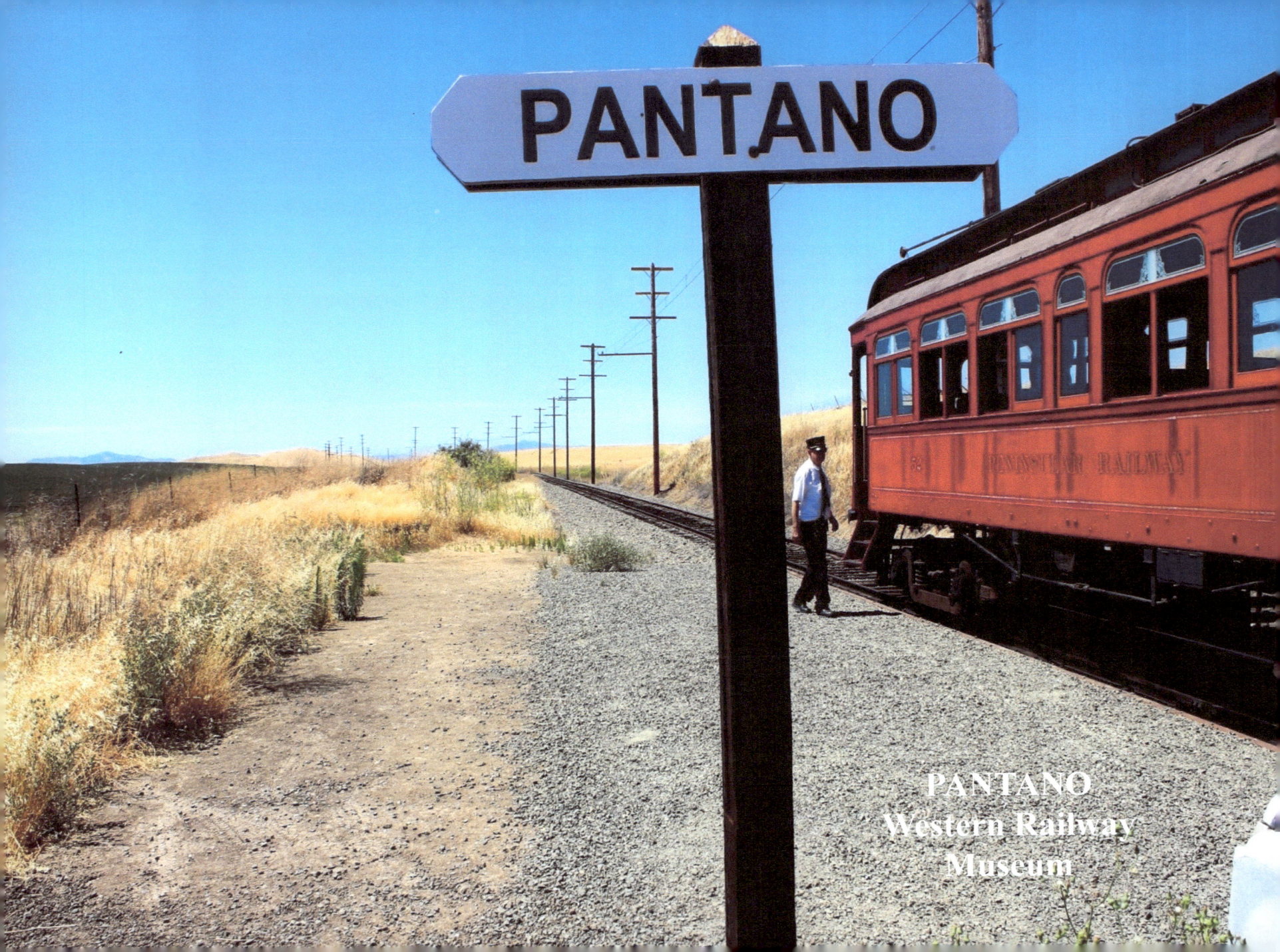

PANTANO
Western Railway
Museum

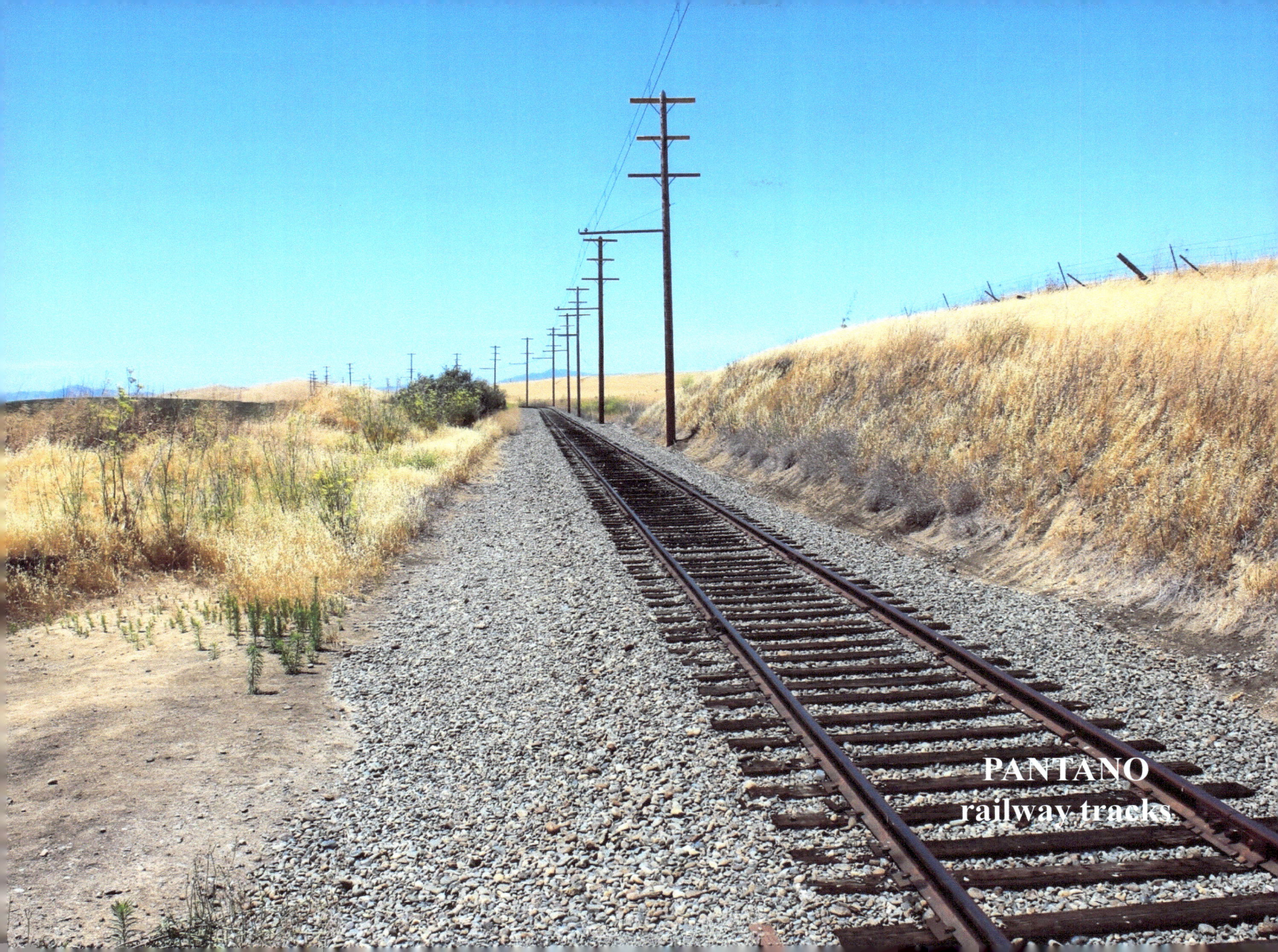

PANTANO
railway tracks

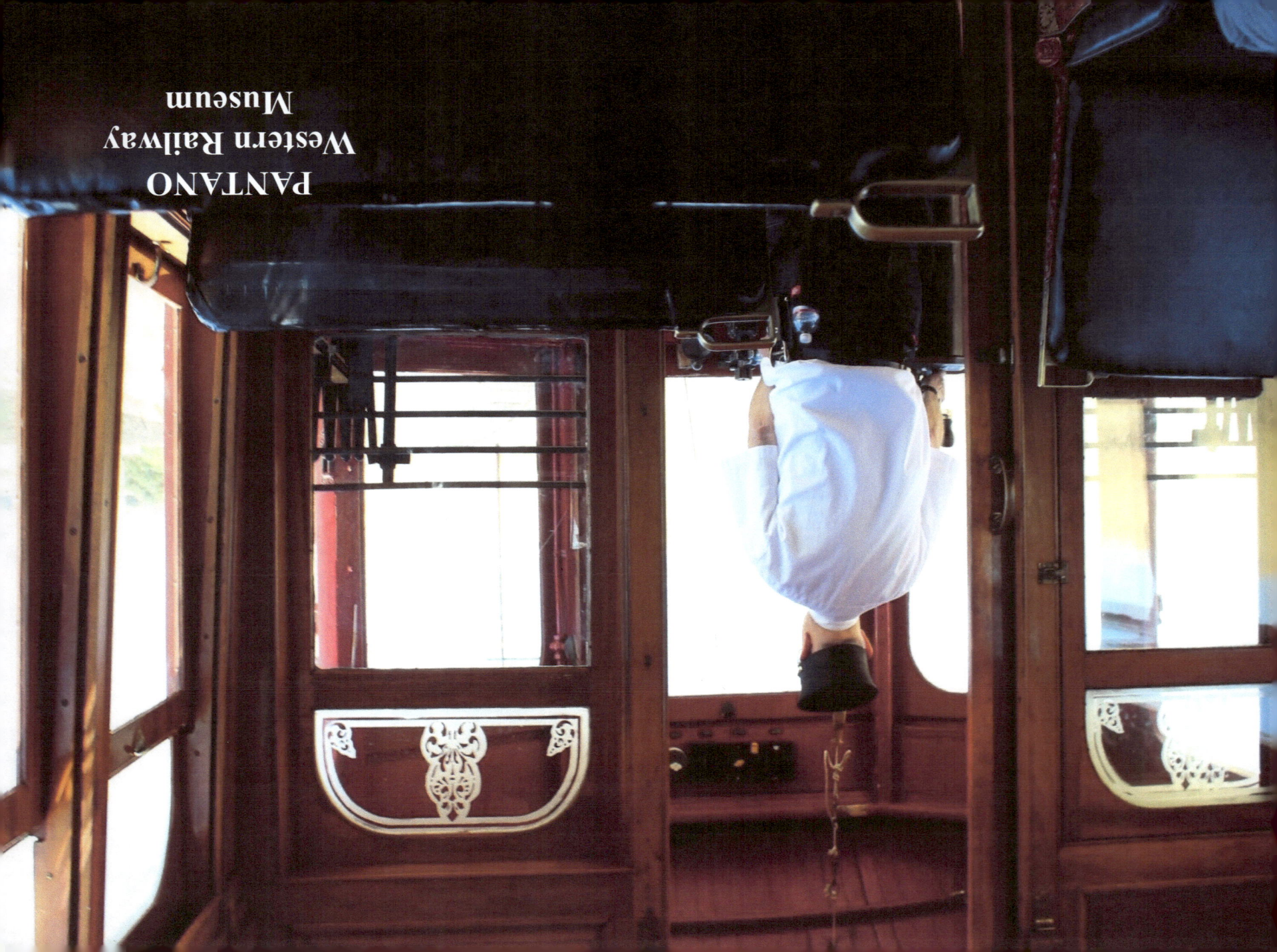

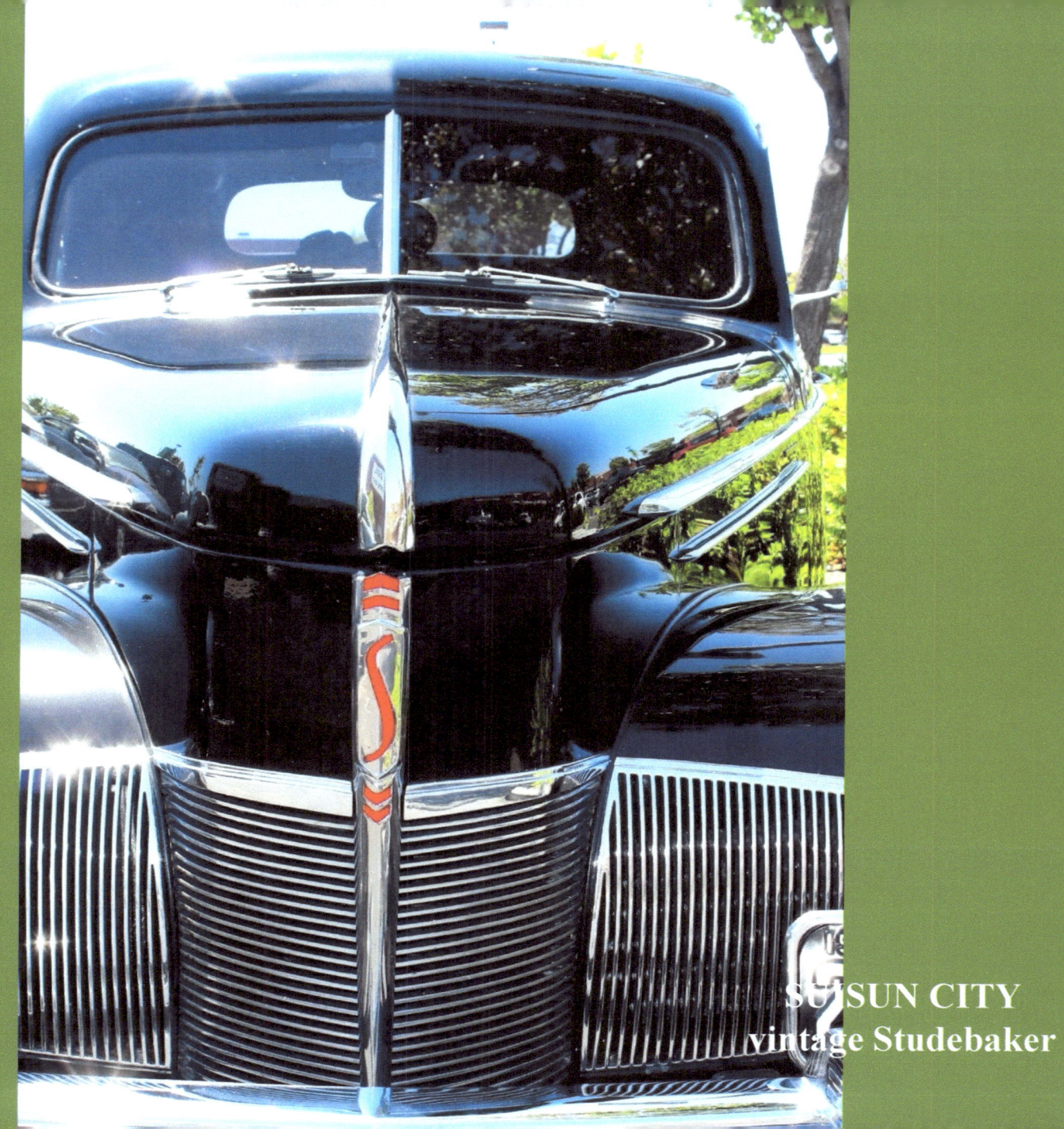

SUISUN CITY
vintage Studebaker

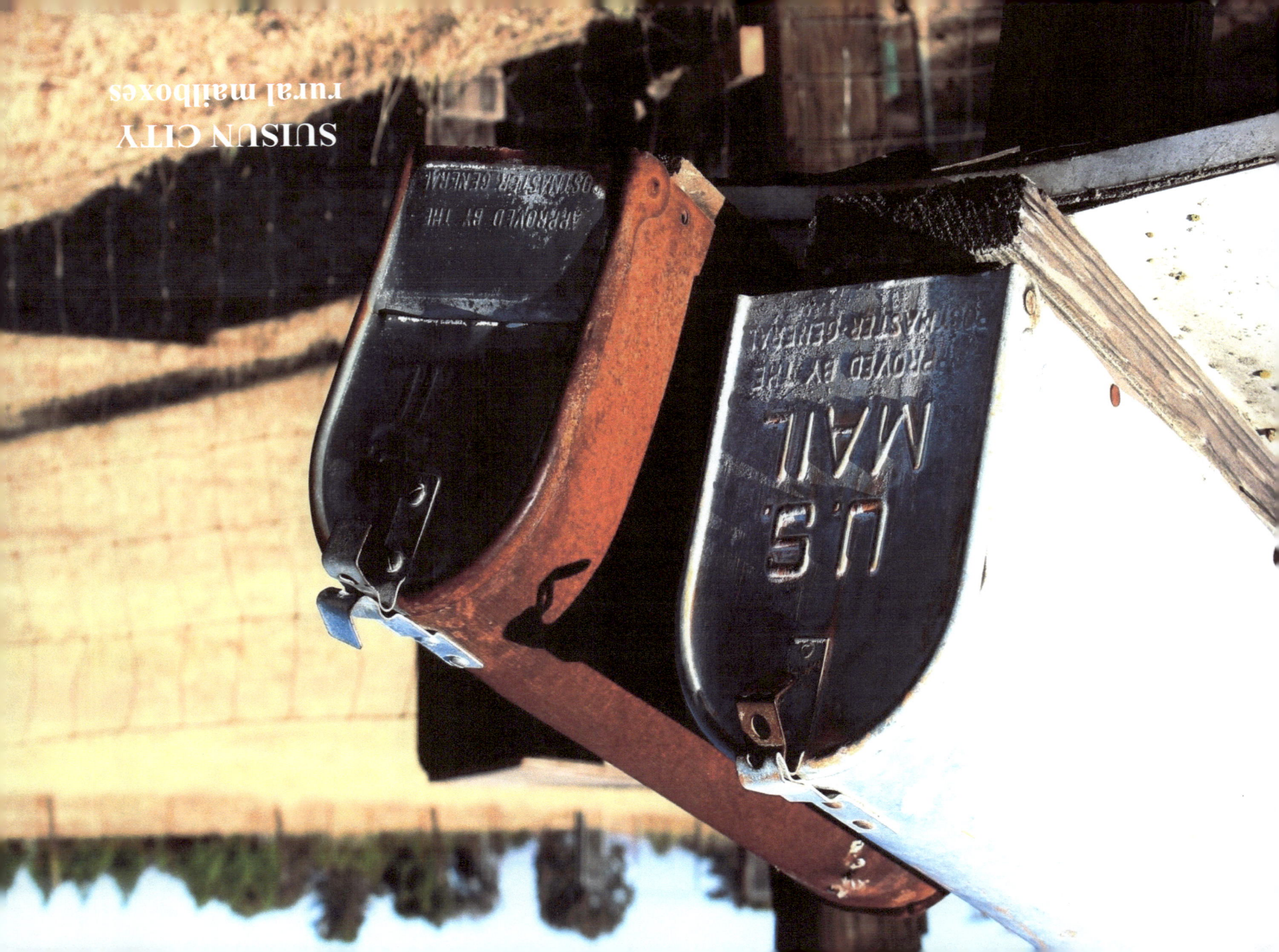

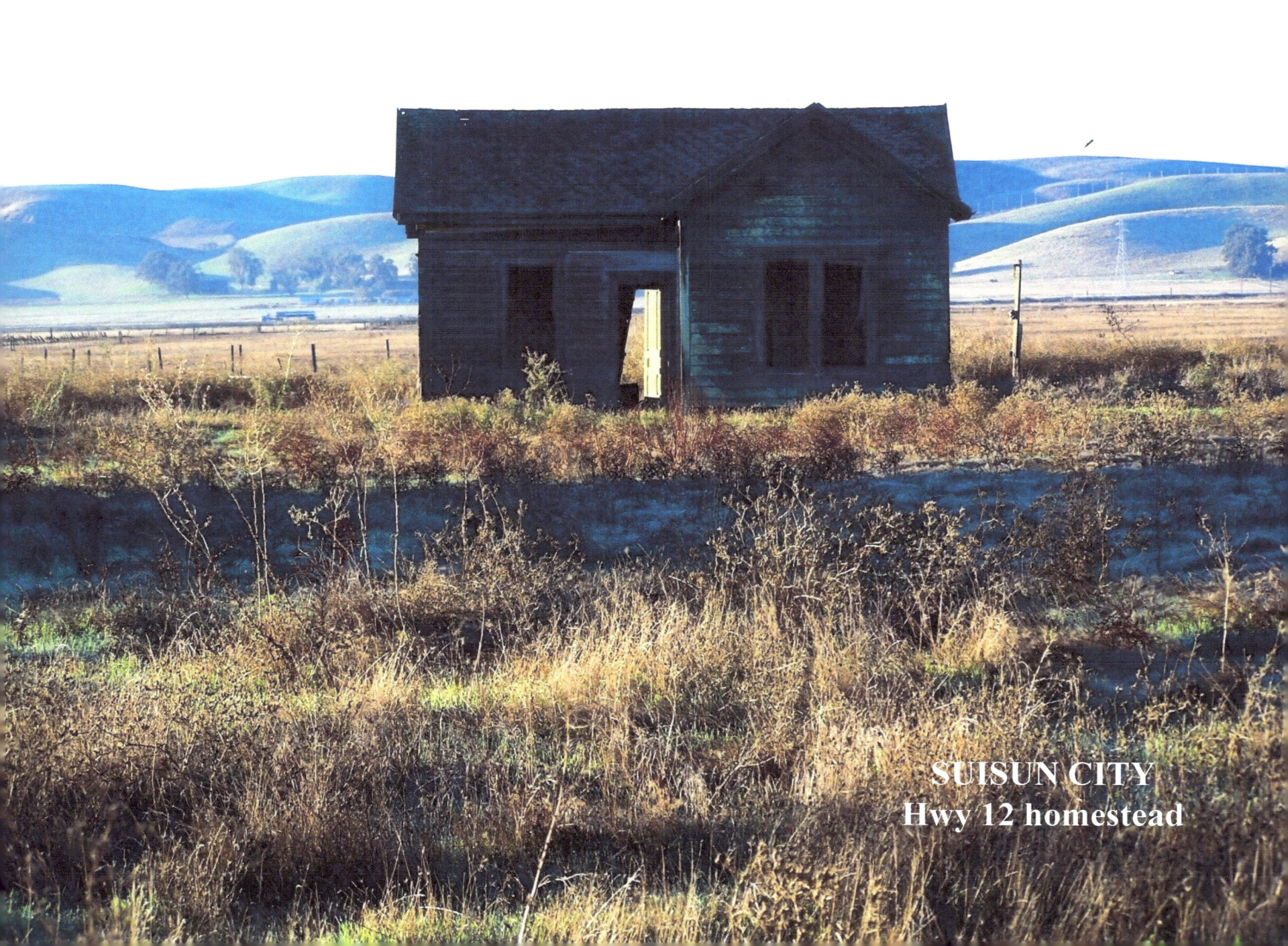

SUISUN CITY
Hwy 12 homestead

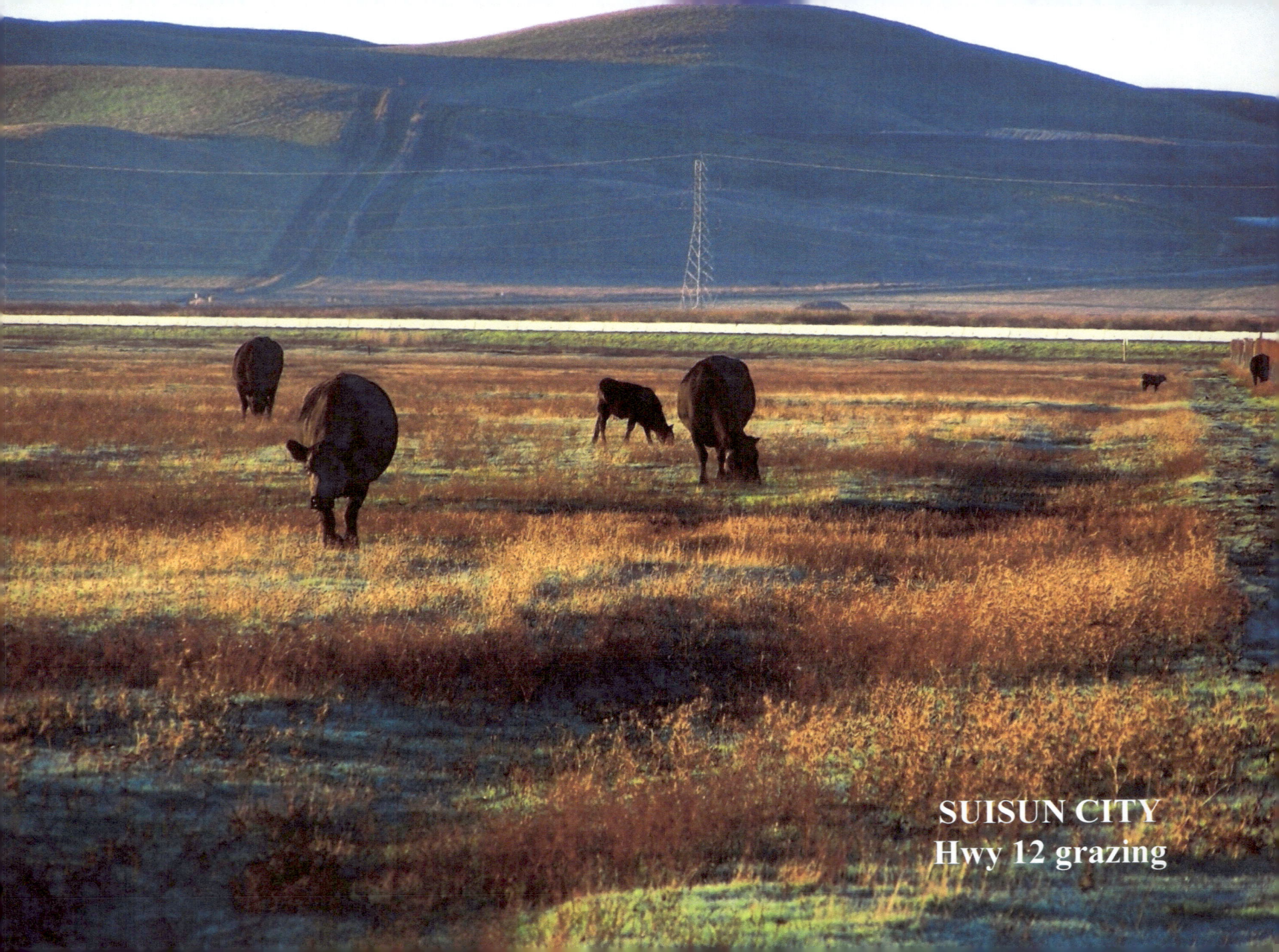

SUISUN CITY
Hwy 12 grazing

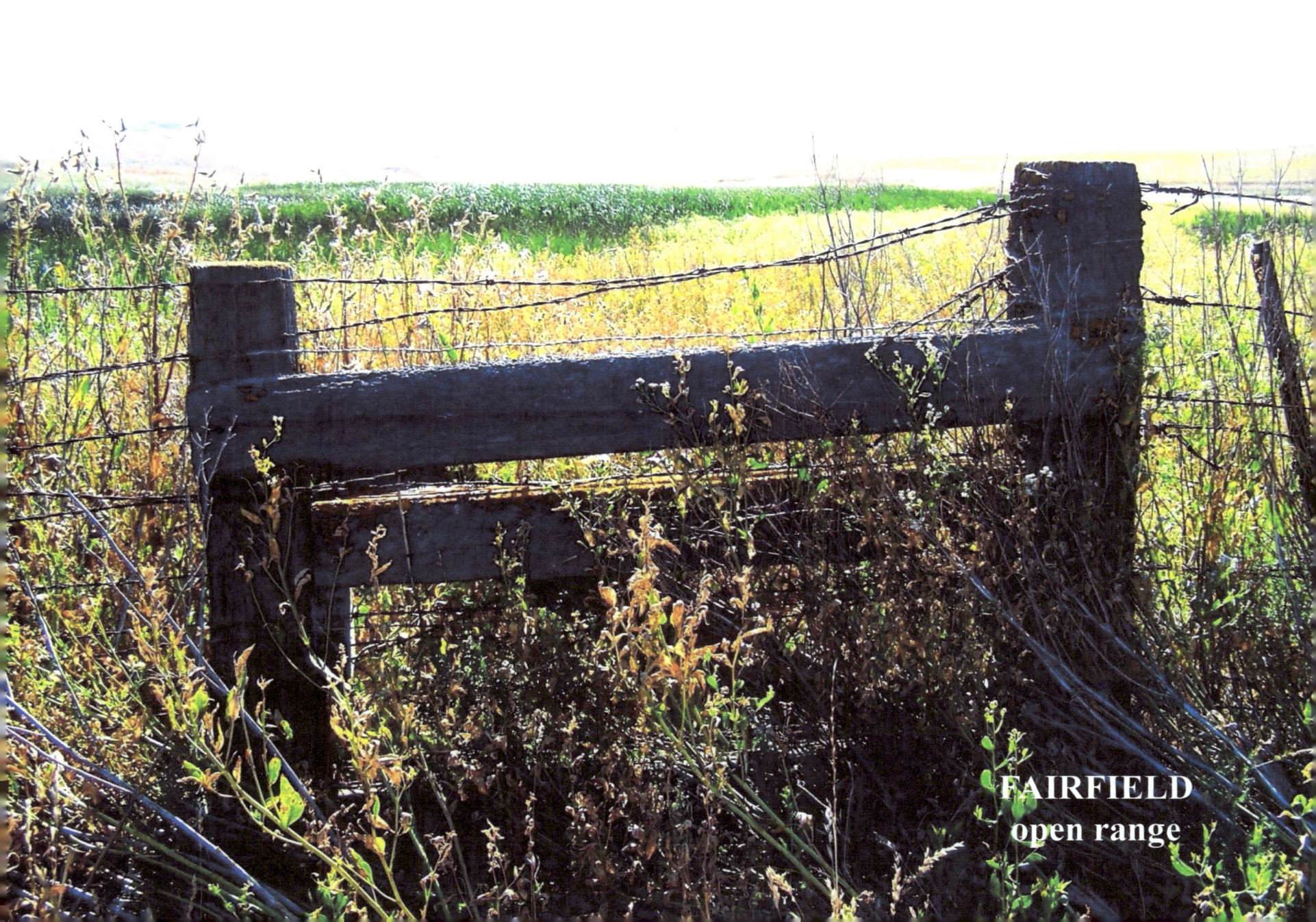

FAIRFIELD
open range

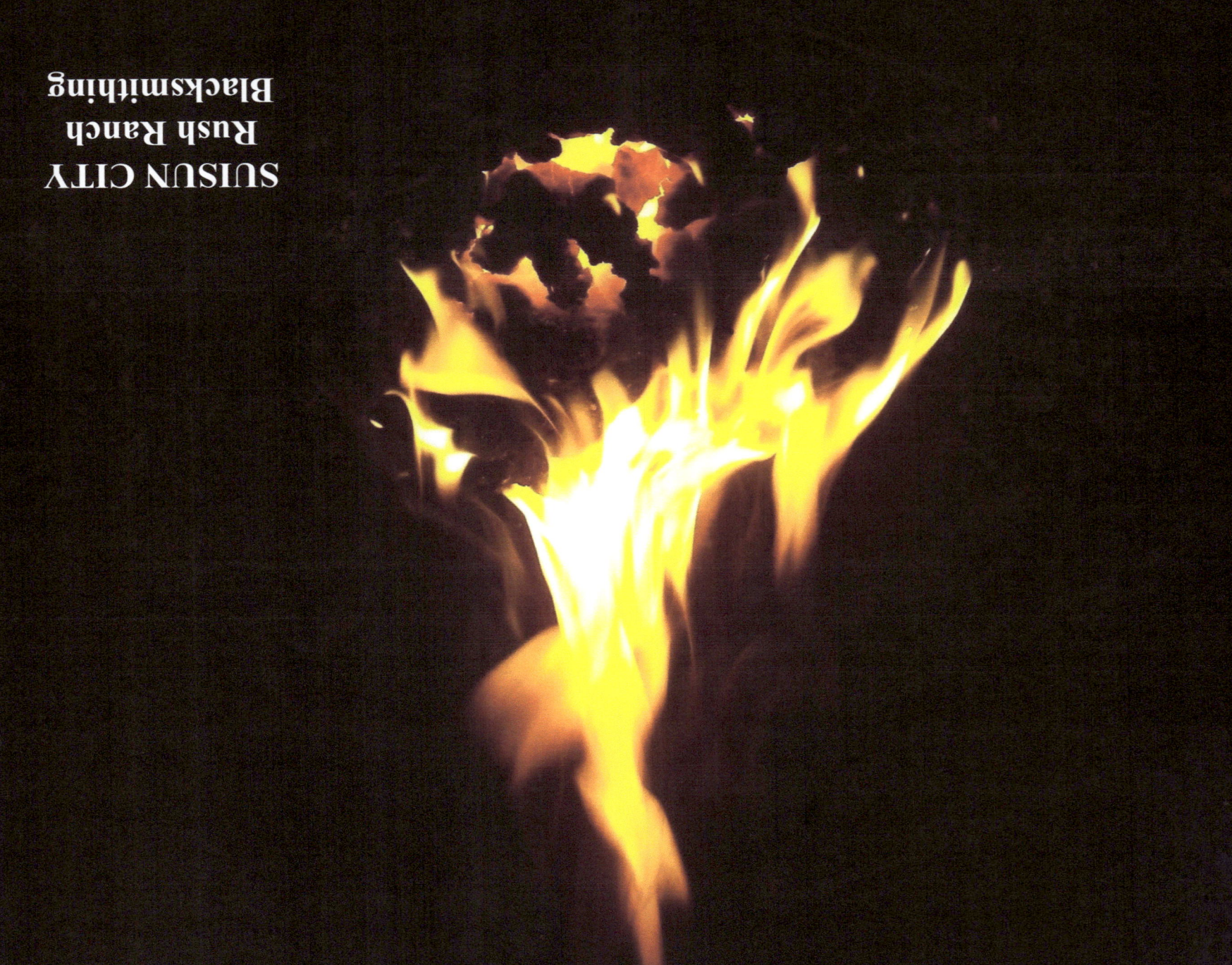

SUISUN CITY
Rush Ranch
Blacksmithing

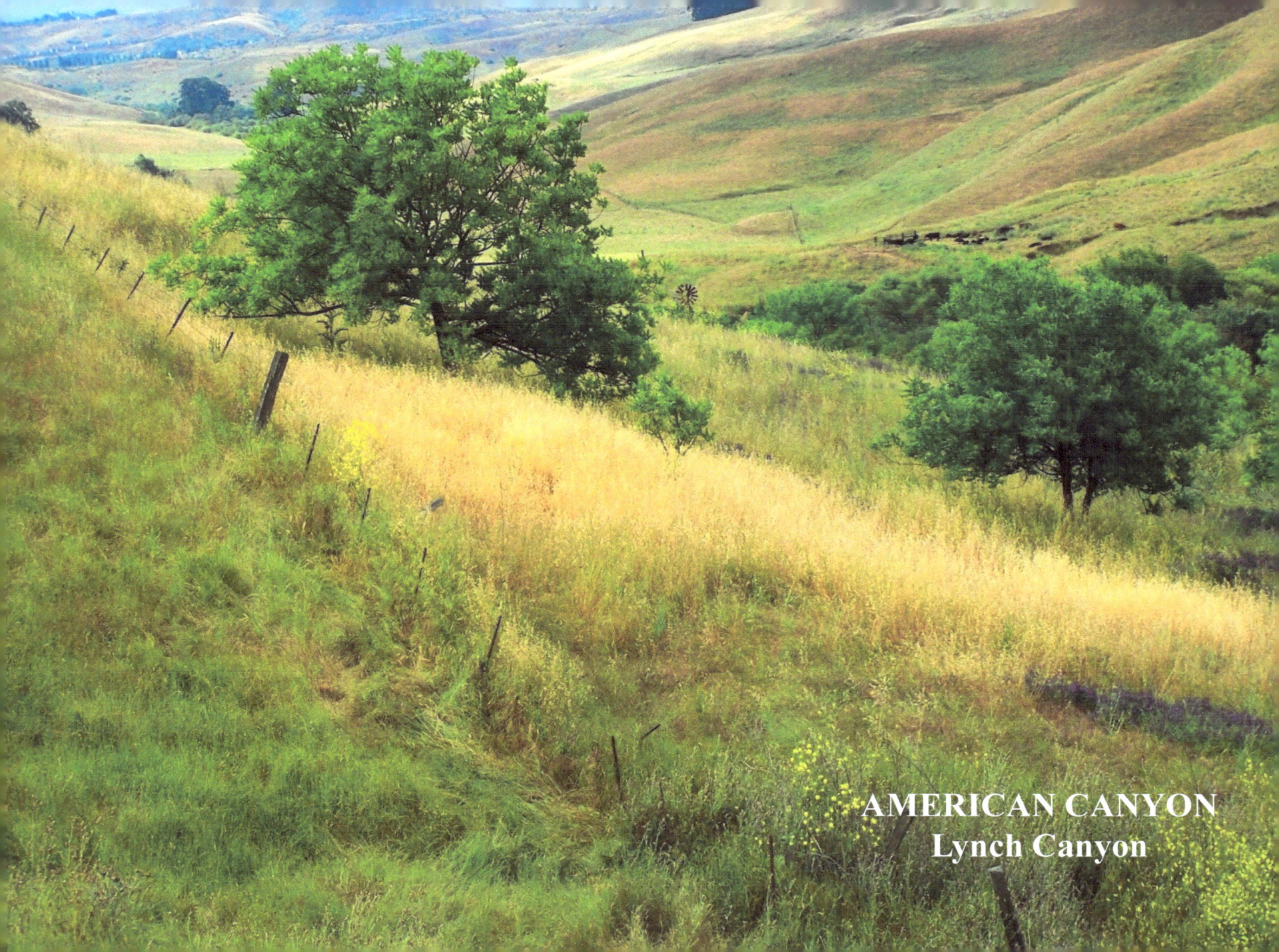

AMERICAN CANYON
Lynch Canyon

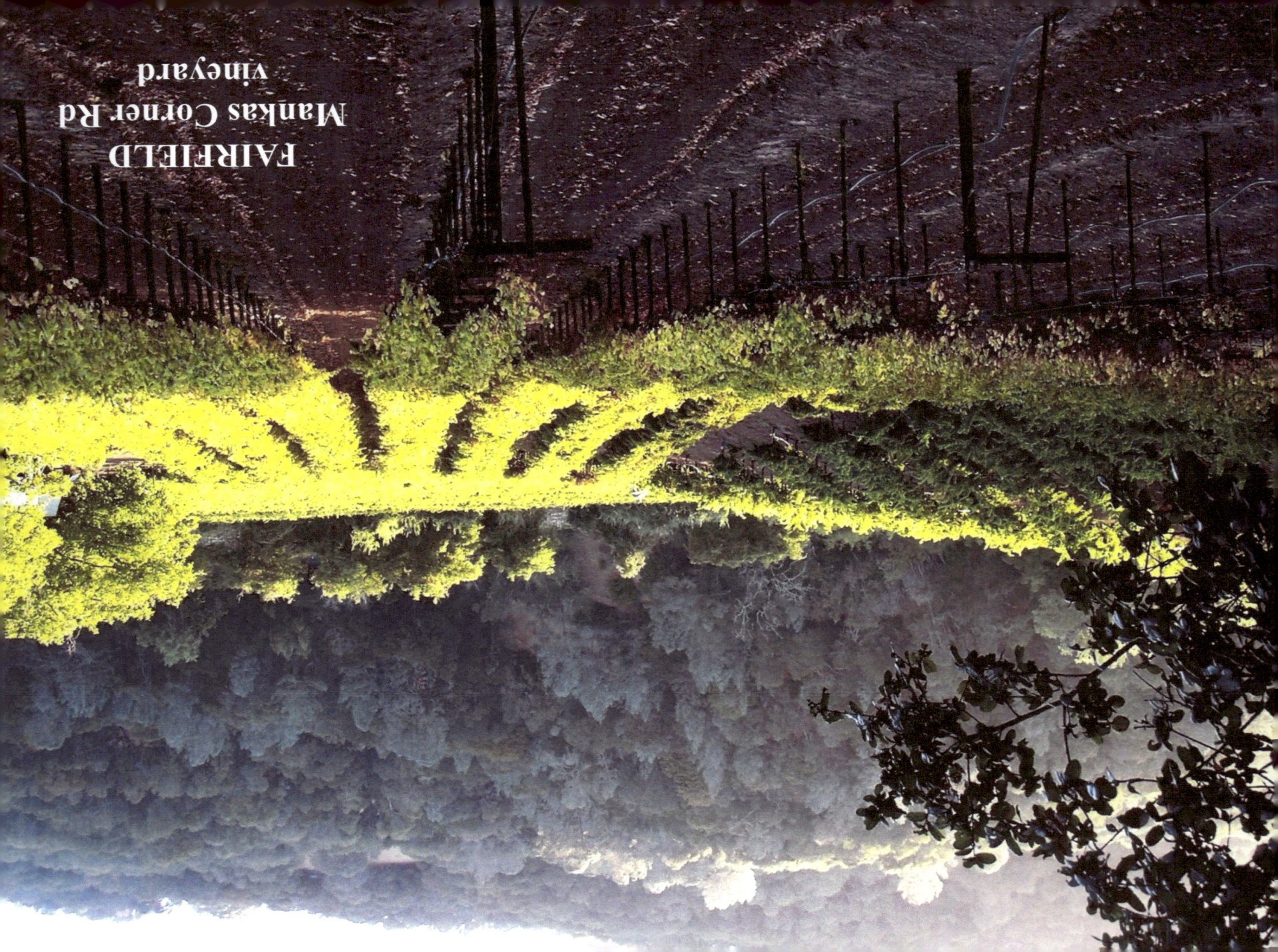

FAIRFIELD
Mankas Corner Rd
vineyard

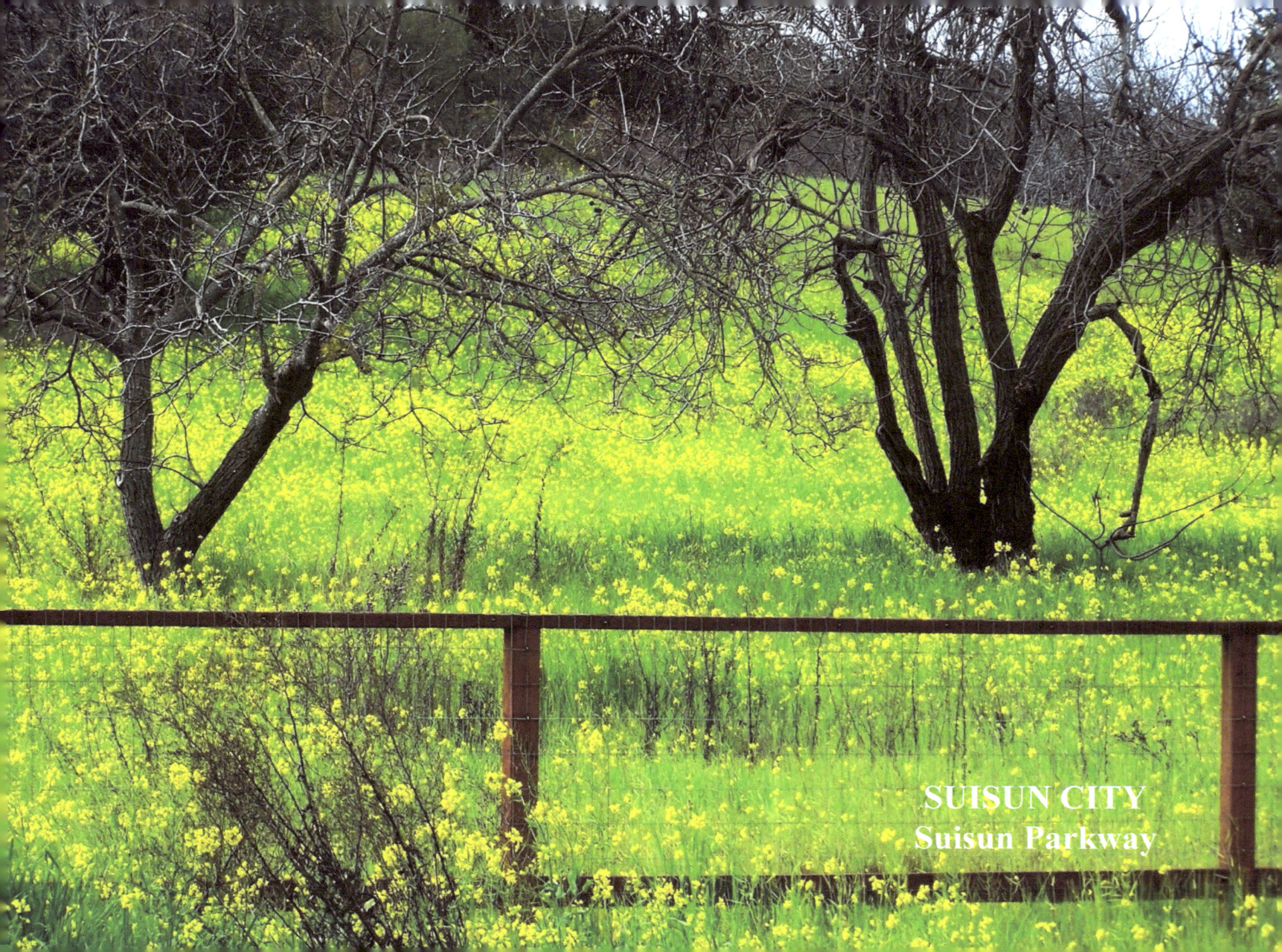

SUISUN CITY
Suisun Parkway

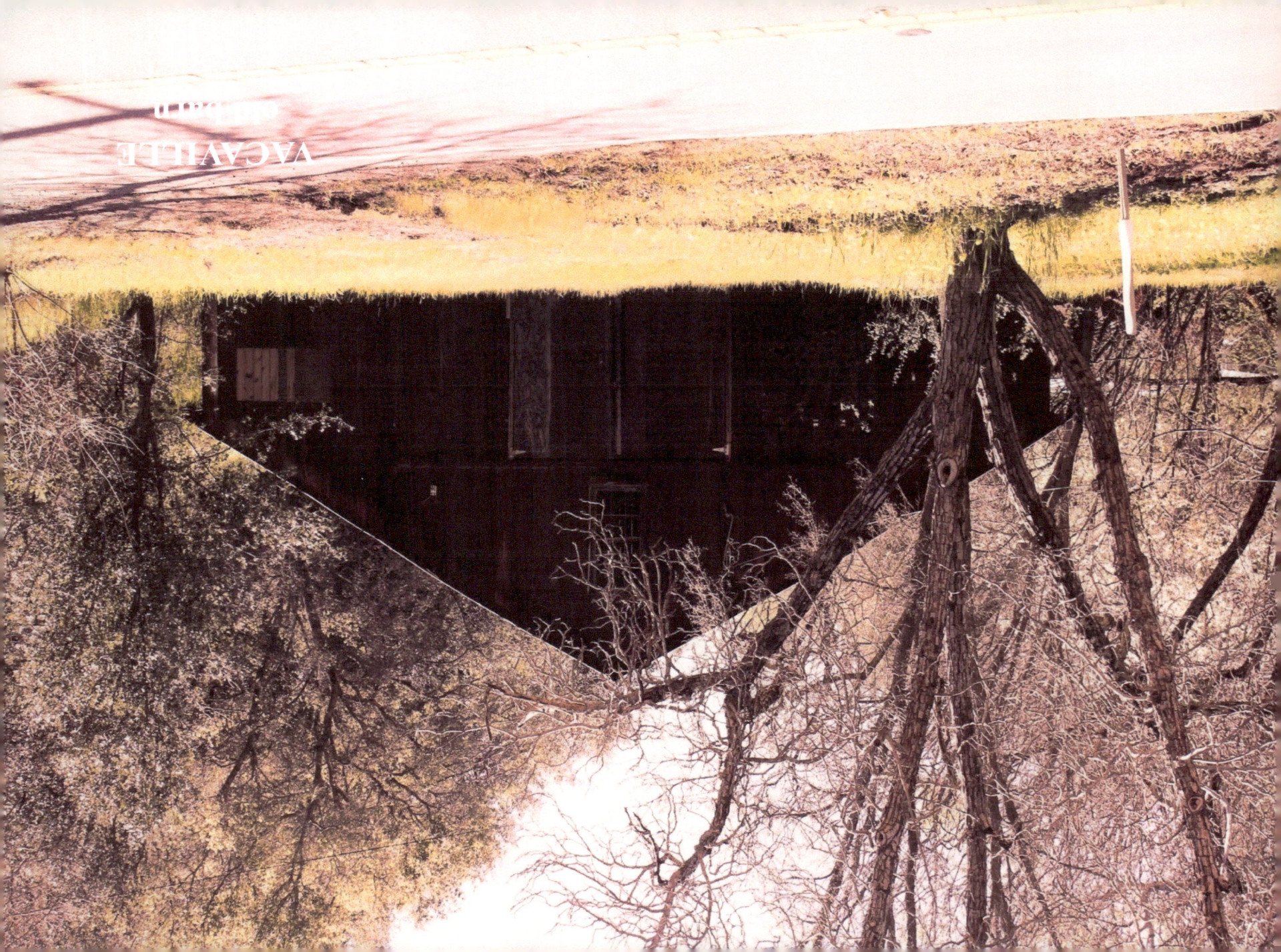

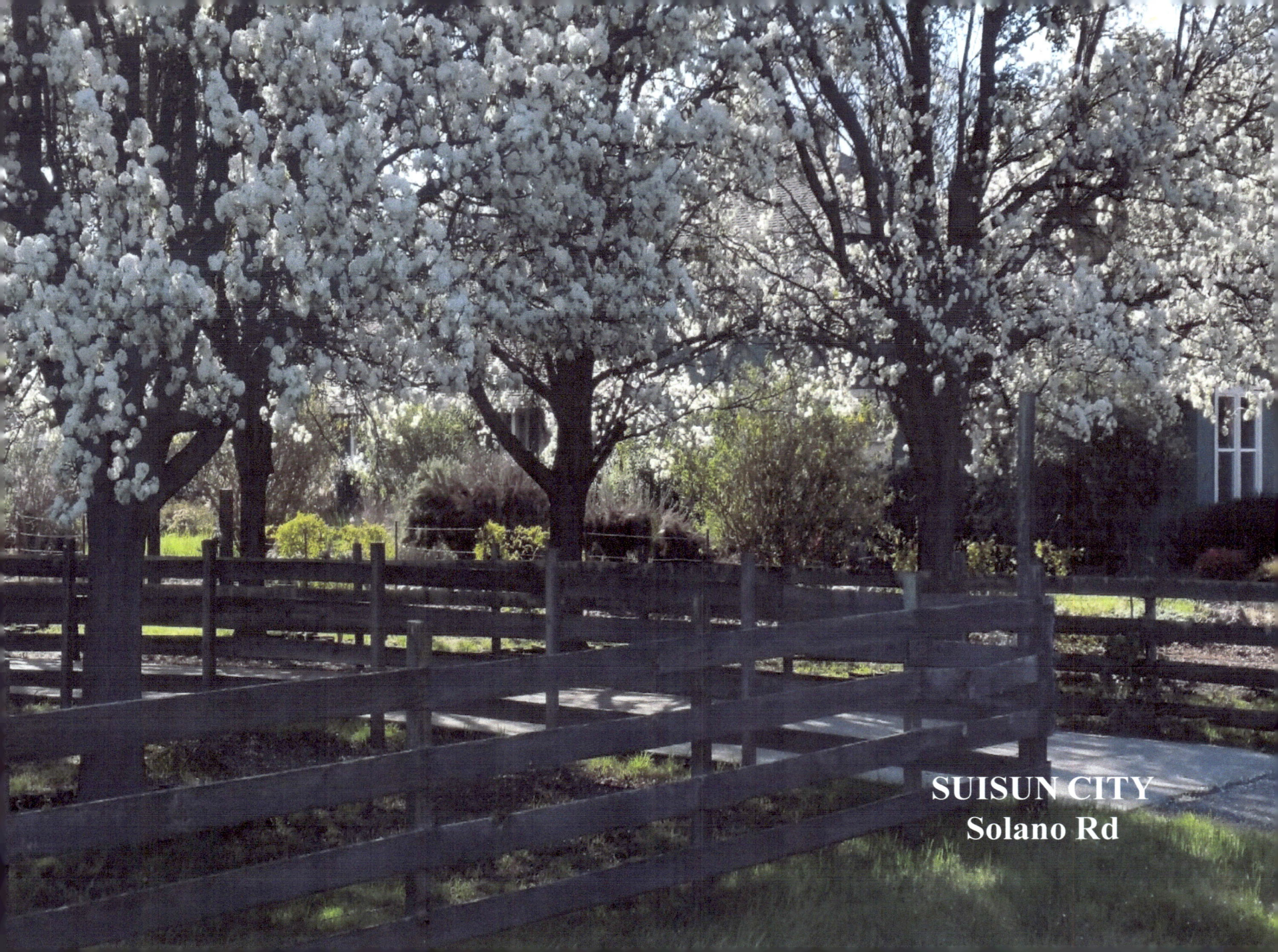

SUISUN CITY
Solano Rd

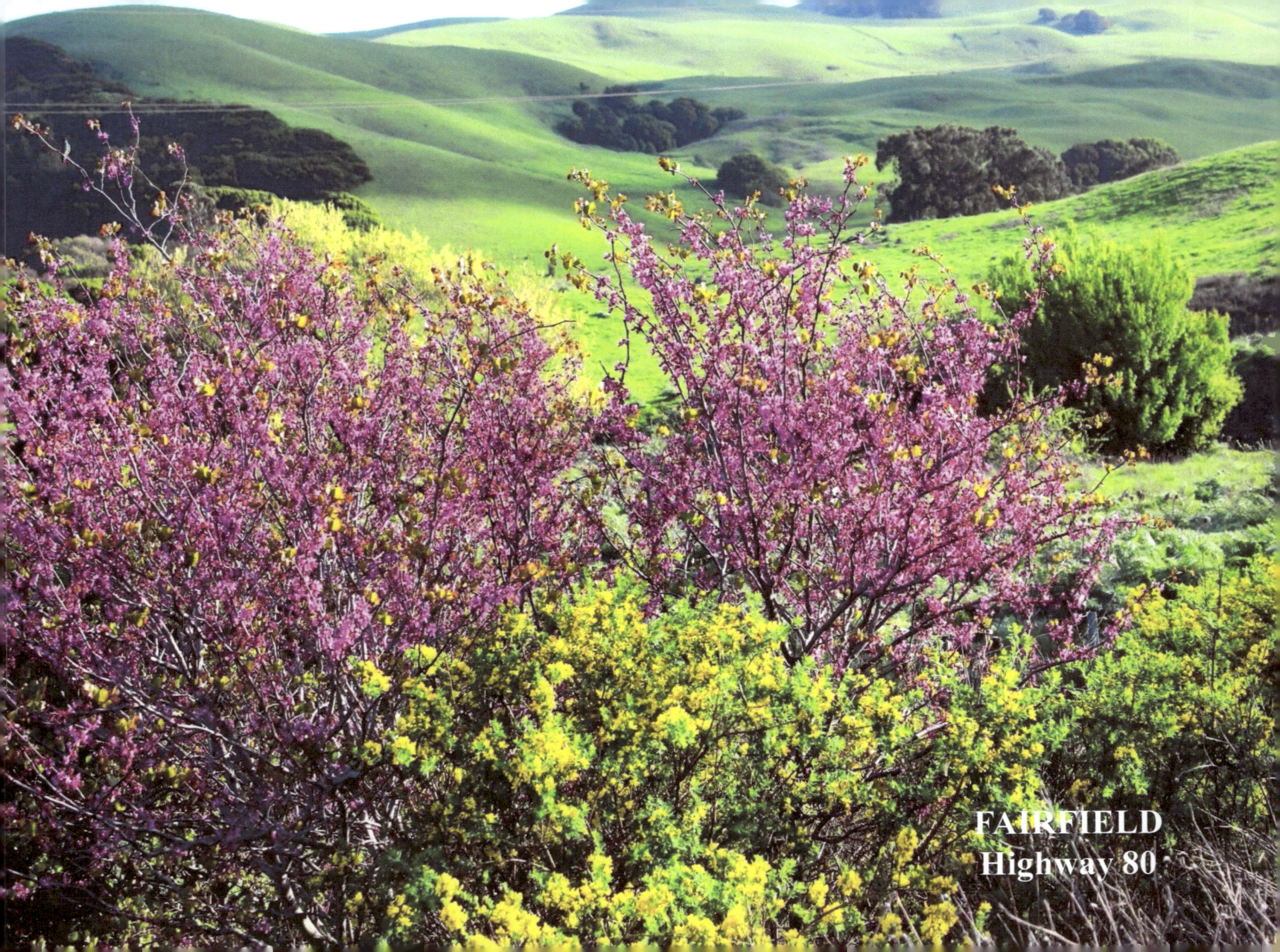

FAIRFIELD
Highway 80

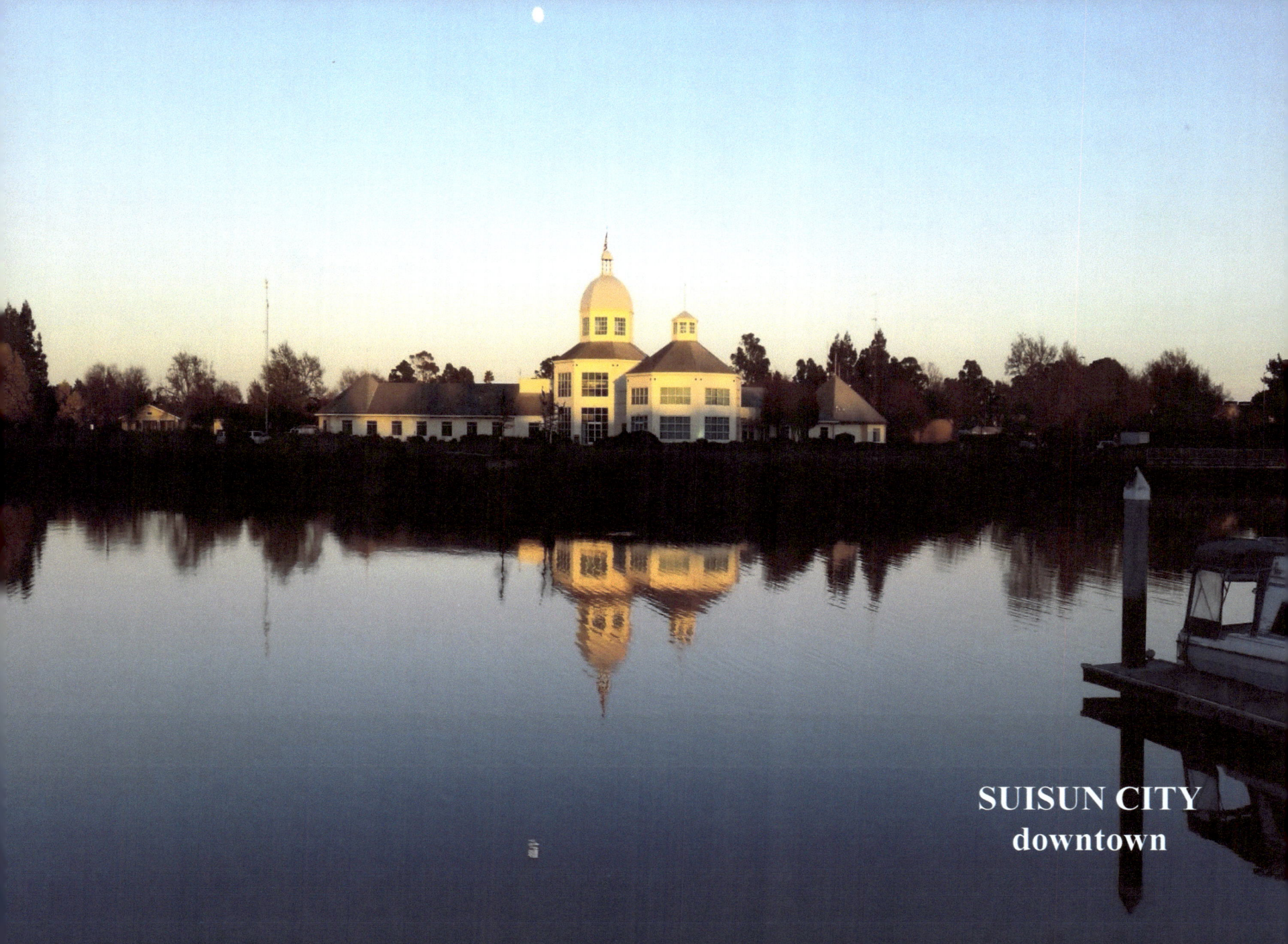

SUISUN CITY
downtown

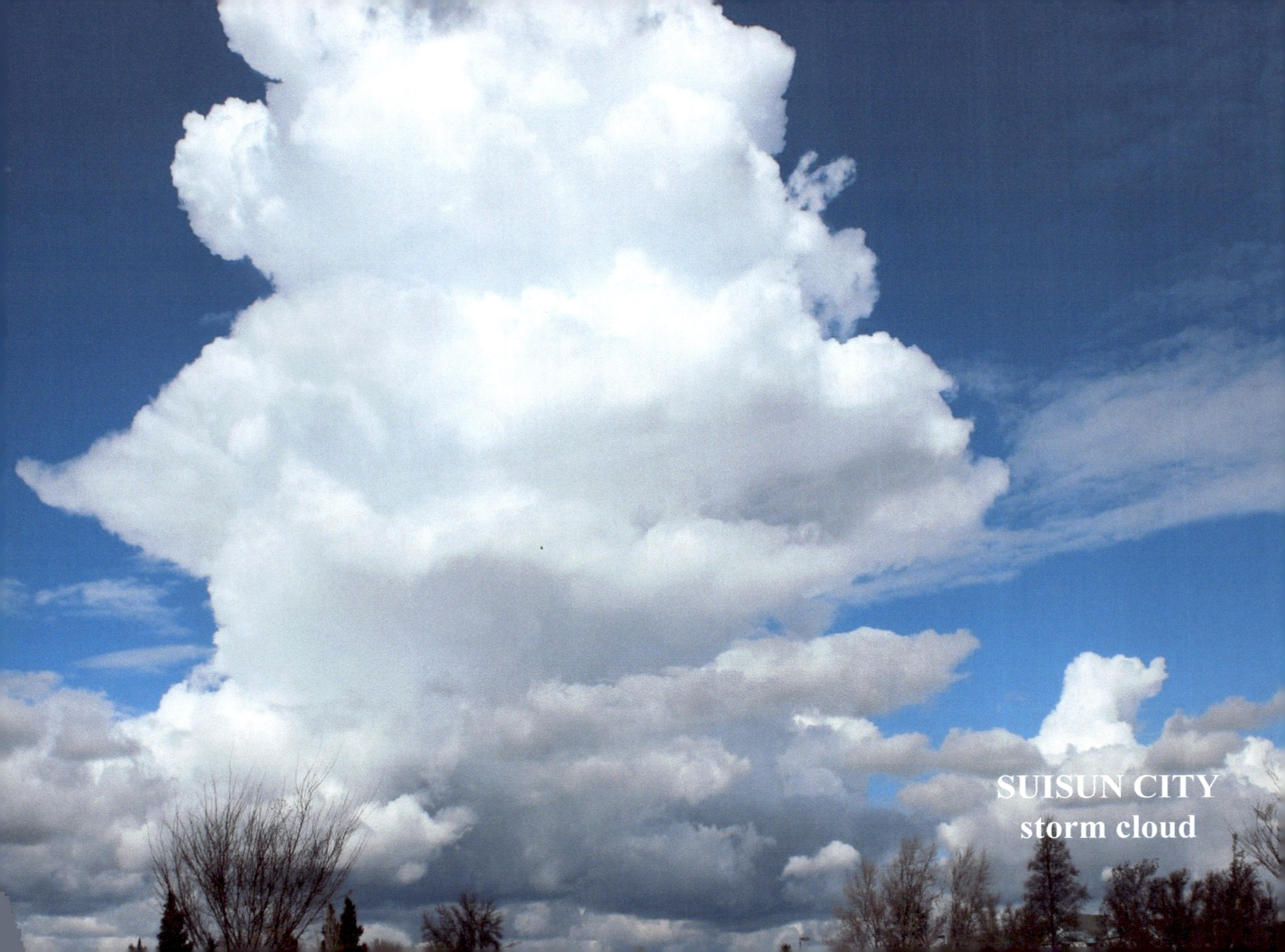

SUISUN CITY
storm cloud

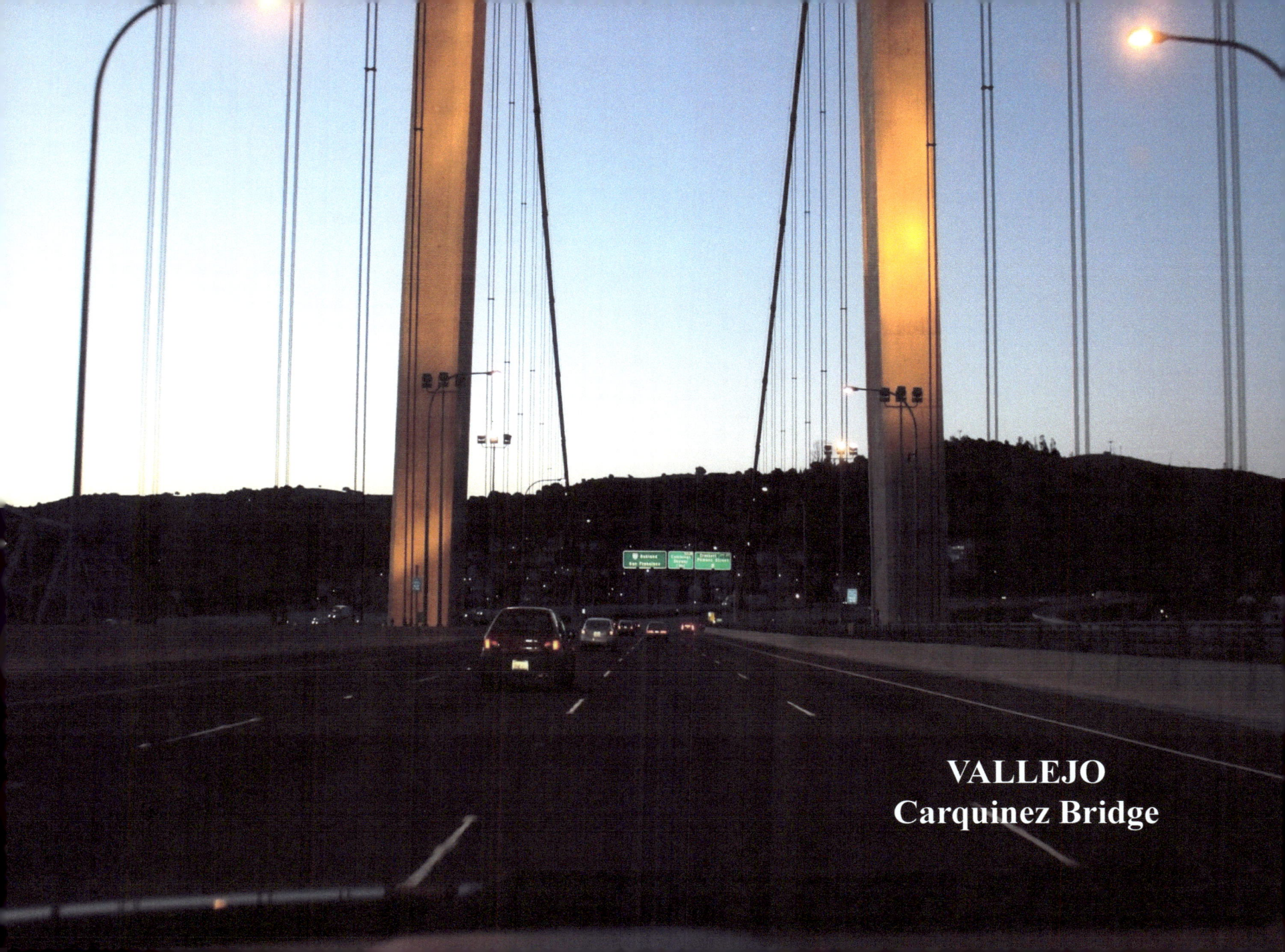

VALLEJO
Carquinez Bridge

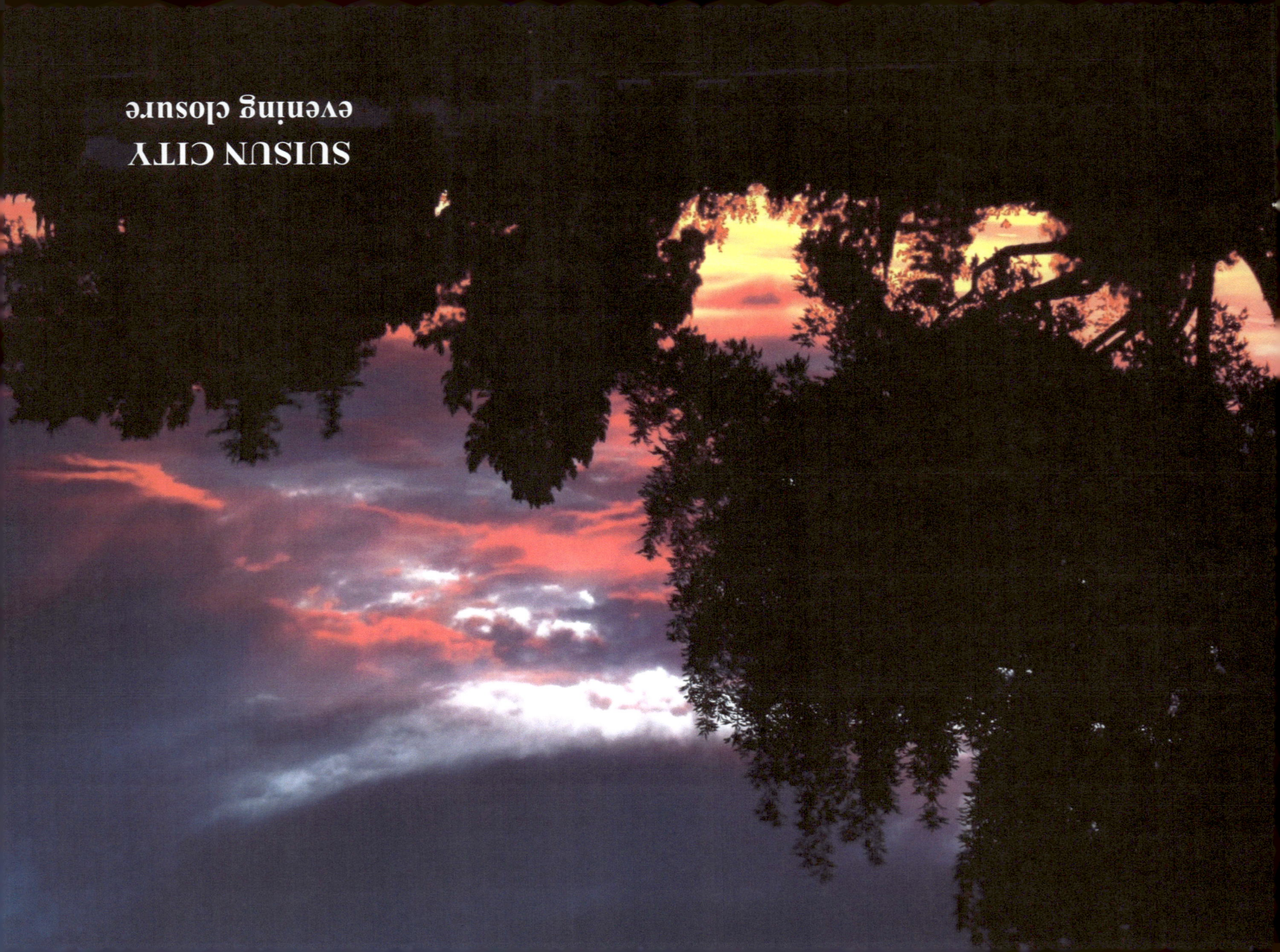

SUISUN CITY
evening closure

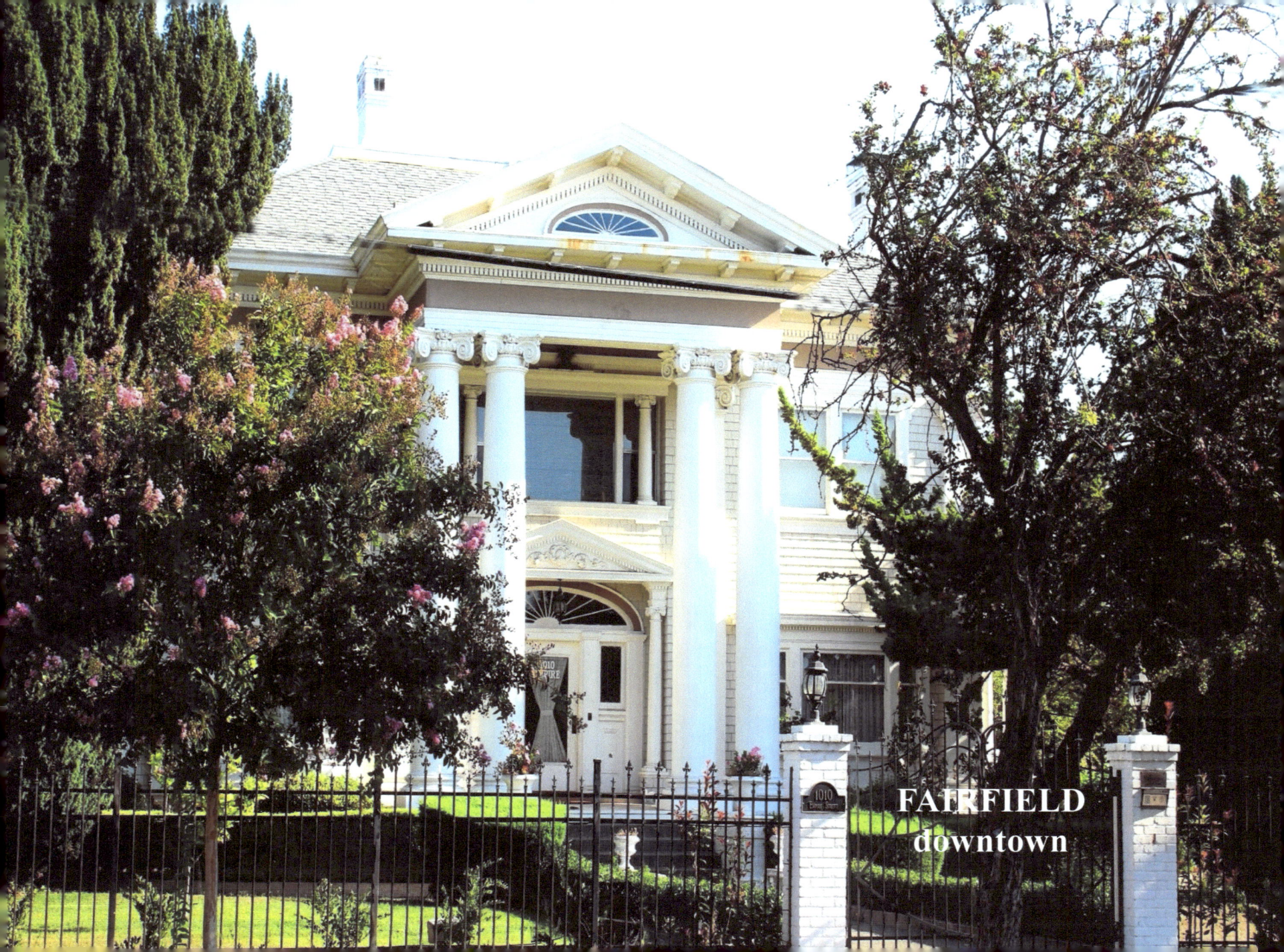

FAIRFIELD
downtown

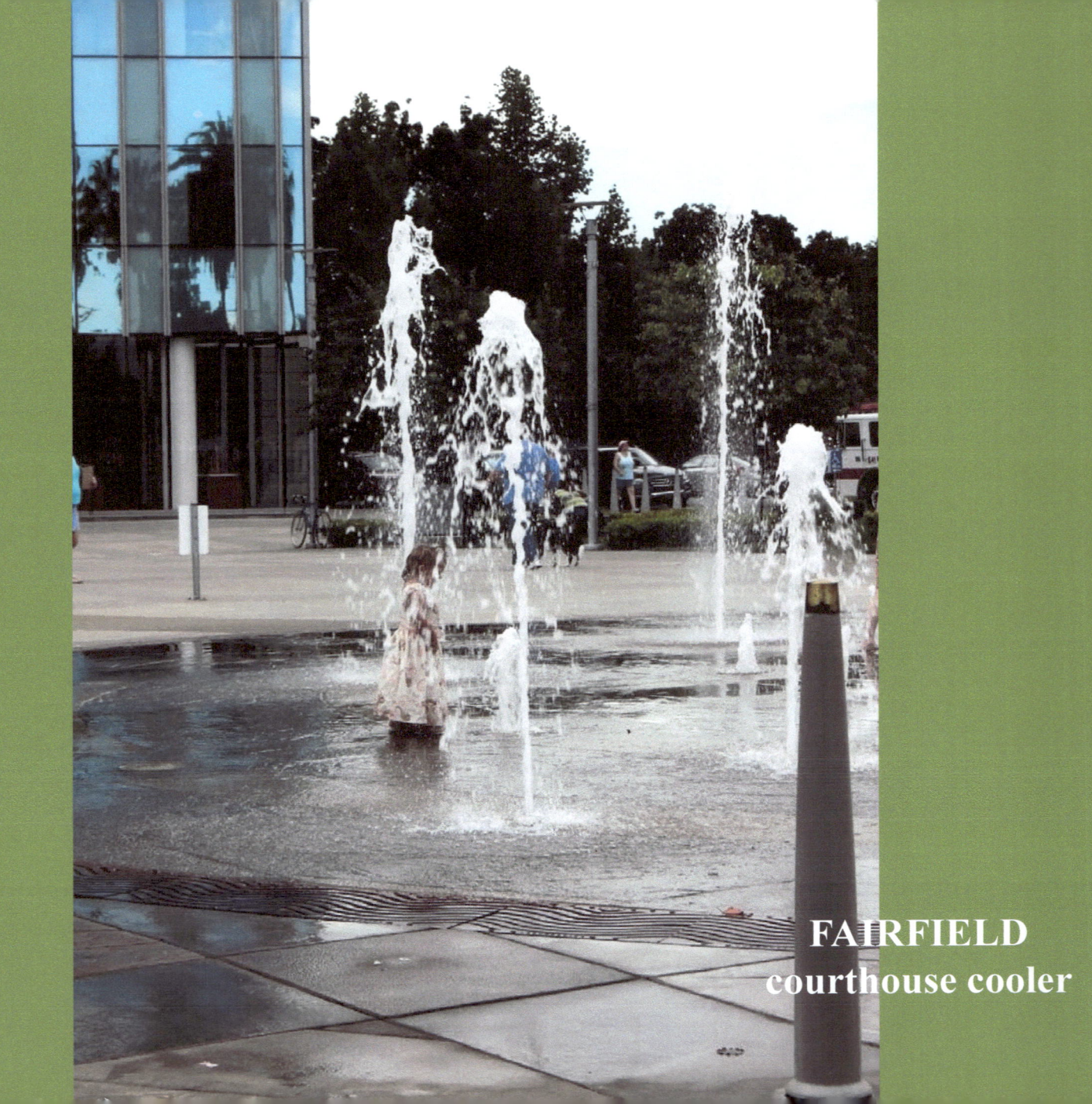

FAIRFIELD
courthouse cooler

About the Author

Sharon Chestang-Robinson is a self-taught artist inspired by her parents who both seemed to know how to create something out of nothing. Her work has become an irreplaceable part of her life. Even though academia and survival had become huge distractions early in life, having been home-schooled was the most ingenious way for her learning. The distractions of life took her away from her best love – art, but she always knew she would return. She returned to art as a way of life in 1989, never to have it leave her side again. Always complimented that her artwork looked 'white' was not a deterrent, but allowed her to persevere as an independent artist, reminding her where her heart was. Native born in the Bay Area of Northern California, she established her studio in 2009 in Suisun City, allowing her to sell her work on commission. She loves to tutor and particularly enjoys teaching miniatures. With art being maintained on a part-time basis since 1989, and after having retired from government in 2016, Sharon now works 9 – 10 hours in her studio gallery. When asked how she feels about her artwork, Sharon comments, "having met celebrity artists over time, I am humbled to have the support of a husband. And the Great Mystery who has placed talented artists in my path, and has guided me throughout so many years of work. I appreciate the number of artworks purchased over the years, and am honored to have my work in homes and businesses, both within America and overseas. Art is a tool that I shall always cherish and be thankful for."

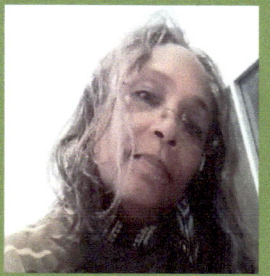